Excel® 2013

FOR

DUMMIES®

A Wiley Brand

PORTABLE EDITION

by Greg Harvey, PhD

FOR

DUMMIES®

A Wiley Brand

Excel® 2013 For Dummies® Portable Edition

Published by
John Wiley & Sons, Inc.
111 River Street
Hoboken, NJ 07030-5774

www.wiley.com

For general information on our other products and services, please contact our Customer Care Department within the U.S. at 877-762-2974, outside the U.S. at 317-572-3993, or fax 317-572-4002.

For technical support, please visit www.wiley.com/techsupport.

Wiley publishes in a variety of print and electronic formats and by print-on-demand. Some material included with standard print versions of this book may not be included in e-books or in print-on-demand. If this book refers to media such as a CD or DVD that is not included in the version you purchased, you may download this material at http://booksupport.wiley.com. For more information about Wiley products, visit www.wiley.com.

Library of Congress Control Number: 2013933945

ISBN 978-1-118- 53438-0 (pbk), 978-1-118-55982-6 (ebk), 978-1-118-55989-5 (ebk), 978-1-118-55990-1 (ebk)

Manufactured in the United States of America

10 9 8 7 6 5 4 3 2 1

About the Author

Greg Harvey has authored tons of computer books, the most recent and most popular being *Excel 2010 For Dummies* and *Excel 2010 All-in-One For Dummies*. He started out training business users on how to use IBM personal computers and their attendant computer software in the rough and tumble days of DOS, WordStar, and Lotus 1-2-3 in the mid-80s of the last century. After working for a number of independent training firms, Greg went on to teach semester-long courses in spreadsheet and database management software at Golden Gate University in San Francisco.

His love of teaching has translated into an equal love of writing. *For Dummies* books are, of course, his all-time favorites to write because they enable him to write to his favorite audience: the beginner. They also enable him to use humor (a key element to success in the training room) and, most delightful of all, to express an opinion or two about the subject matter at hand.

Greg received his doctorate degree in Humanities in Philosophy and Religion with a concentration in Asian Studies and Comparative Religion last May. Everyone is glad that Greg was finally able to get out of school before he retired.

Dedication

An Erucolindo melindonya

Author's Acknowledgments

Let me take this opportunity to thank all the people, both at John Wiley & Sons, Inc., and at Mind over Media, whose dedication and talent combined to get this book out and into your hands in such great shape.

At John Wiley & Sons, Inc., I want to thank Andy Cummings and Katie Feltman for their encouragement and help in getting this project underway and their ongoing support every step of the way. These people made sure that the project stayed on course and made it into production so that all the talented folks on the production team could create this great final product.

At Mind over Media, I want to thank Christopher Aiken for his review of the updated manuscript and invaluable input and suggestions on how best to restructure the book to accommodate all the wonderful new features in Excel 2013 and, more importantly, layout the exciting new "anytime, anywhere" story to Excel users.

Publisher's Acknowledgments

We're proud of this book; please send us your comments at http://dummies. custhelp.com. For other comments, please contact our Customer Care Department within the U.S. at 877-762-2974, outside the U.S. at 317-572-3993, or fax 317-572-4002.

Some of the people who helped bring this book to market include the following:

Acquisitions and Editorial

Senior Project Editor: Nicole Sholly

Acquisitions Editor: Constance Santisteban

Copy Editors: Amanda Graham, Jean Nelson

Technical Editor: Russ Mullen

Editorial Manager: Kevin Kirschner

Editorial Assistant: Anne Sullivan

Sr. Editorial Assistant: Cherie Case

Cover Photo: © teekid / iStockphoto

Composition Services

Senior Project Coordinator: Kristie Rees

Layout and Graphics: Jennifer Creasey, Joyce Haughey

Proofreader: Cynthia Fields

Indexer: Potomac Indexing, LLC

Publishing and Editorial for Technology Dummies

Richard Swadley, Vice President and Executive Group Publisher

Andy Cummings, Vice President and Publisher

Mary Bednarek, Executive Acquisitions Director

Mary C. Corder, Editorial Director

Publishing for Consumer Dummies

Kathleen Nebenhaus, Vice President and Executive Publisher

Composition Services

Debbie Stailey, Director of Composition Services

Table of Contents

Introduction

● ●

I'm very proud to present you with *Excel 2013 For Dummies,* Portable Edition, the latest version of everybody's favorite book on Microsoft Office Excel for readers with no intention whatsoever of becoming spreadsheet gurus.

Excel 2013 For Dummies, Portable Edition, covers all the fundamental techniques you need to know in order to create, edit, format, and print your own worksheets. In addition to showing you around the worksheet, this book also exposes you to automating, linking, and sharing spreadsheets.This book concentrates on spreadsheets because spreadsheets are what most regular folks create with Excel.

About This Book

This book isn't meant to be read cover to cover. Although its chapters are loosely organized in a logical order (progressing as you might when studying Excel in a classroom situation), each topic covered in a chapter is really meant to stand on its own.

Each discussion of a topic briefly addresses the question of what a particular feature is good for before launching into how to use it. In Excel, as with most other sophisticated programs, you usually have more than one way to do a task. For the sake of your sanity, I have purposely limited the choices by usually giving you only the most efficient ways to do a particular task. Later, if you're so tempted, you can experiment with alternative ways of doing a task. For now, just concentrate on performing the task as I describe.

As much as possible, I've tried to make it unnecessary for you to remember anything covered in another section of the book. From time to time, however, you will come across a cross-reference to another section or chapter in the book. For the most part, such cross-references are meant to help you get more complete information on a subject, should you have the time and interest. If you have neither, no problem. Just ignore the cross-references as if they never existed.

How to Use This Book

This book is similar to a reference book. You can start by looking up the topic you need information about (in either the Table of Contents or the index) and then refer directly to the section of interest. I explain most topics conversationally (as though you were sitting in the back of a classroom where you can safely nap). Sometimes, however, my regiment-commander mentality takes over, and I list the steps you need to take to accomplish a particular task in a particular section.

What You Can Safely Ignore

When you come across a section that contains the steps you take to get something done, you can safely ignore all text accompanying the steps (the text that isn't in bold) if you have neither the time nor the inclination to wade through more material.

Whenever possible, I have also tried to separate background or footnote-type information from the essential facts by exiling this kind of junk to a sidebar (look for blocks of text on a gray background). Often, these sections are flagged with icons that let you know what type of information you will encounter there. You can easily disregard text marked this way. (I'll scoop you on the icons I use in this book a little later.)

Foolish Assumptions

I'm only going to make one foolish assumption about you and that is that you have some need to use Microsoft Excel 2013 in your work or studies. If pushed, I further guess that you aren't particularly interested in knowing Excel at an expert level but are terribly motivated to find out how to do the stuff you need to get done. If that's the case, this is definitely the book for you. Fortunately, even if you happen to be one of those newcomers who's highly motivated to become the company's resident spreadsheet guru, you've still come to the right place.

As far as your hardware and software goes, I'm assuming that you already have Excel 2013 (usually as part of Microsoft Office 2013) installed on your computing device, using a standard home or business installation running under either Windows 7 or 8. I'm not assuming, however, that when you're using Excel 2013 under Windows 7 or 8 that you're sitting in front of a large-screen monitor and making cell entries and command selections with a physical keyboard or connected mouse. With the introduction of Microsoft's Surface tablet for Windows 8 and the support for a whole slew of different Windows tablets, you may well be entering data and selecting commands with your finger or stylus using the Windows Touch keyboard and Touch Pointer.

To deal with the differences between using Excel 2013 on a standard desktop or laptop computer with access only to a physical keyboard and mouse and a touchscreen tablet or smartphone environment with access only to the virtual Touch keyboard and Touch Pointer, I've outlined the touchscreen equivalents to common commands you find throughout the text such as "click," "double-click," "drag," and so forth in the section entitled, "Selecting commands by touch" in Chapter 1.

Keep in mind that although most of the figures in this book show Excel 2013 happily running on Windows 7, you will see the occasional figure showing Excel running on Windows 8 in the rare cases (as when opening and saving files) where the operating system you're using does make a difference.

This book is intended *only* for users of Microsoft Excel 2013! Because of the diversity of the devices that Excel 2013 runs on and the places where its files can be saved and used, if you're using Excel 2007 or Excel 2010 for Windows, much of the file-related information in this book may only confuse and confound you. If you're still using a version prior to Excel 2007, which introduced the Ribbon interface, this edition will be of no use to you because your version of the program works nothing like the 2013 version this book describes.

Conventions Used in This Book

The following information gives you the lowdown on how things look in this book. Publishers call these items the book's *conventions* (no campaigning, flag-waving, name-calling, or finger-pointing is involved, however).

Selecting Ribbon commands

Throughout the book, you'll find Ribbon command sequences (the name on the tab on the Ribbon and the command button you select) separated by a command arrow, as in:

HOME⇨Copy

This shorthand is the Ribbon command that copies whatever cells or graphics are currently selected to the Windows Clipboard. It means that you click the Home tab on the Ribbon (if it isn't displayed already) and then click the Copy button (that sports the traditional side-by-side page icon).

Some of the Ribbon command sequences involve not only selecting a command button on a tab, but then also selecting an item on a drop-down menu. In this case, the drop-down menu command follows the name of the tab and command button, all separated by command arrows, as in:

Formulas⇨Calculation Options⇨Manual

This shorthand is the Ribbon command sequence that turns on manual recalculation in Excel. It says that you click the Formulas tab (if it isn't displayed already) and then click the Calculation Options button followed by the Manual drop-down menu option.

The book occasionally encourages you to type something specific into a specific cell in the worksheet. When I tell you to enter a specific function, the part you should type generally appears in **bold** type. For example, **=SUM(A2:B2)** means that you should type exactly what you see: an equal sign, the word **SUM**, a left parenthesis, the text **A2:B2** (complete with a colon between the letter-number combos), and a right parenthesis. You then, of course, have to press Enter to make the entry stick.

Occasionally, I give you a *hot key combination* that you can press in order to choose a command from the keyboard rather than clicking buttons on the Ribbon with the mouse.

Hot key combinations are written like this: Alt+FS or Ctrl+S (both of these hot key combos save workbook changes).

With the Alt key combos on a physical keyboard, you press the Alt key until the hot key letters appear in little squares all along the Ribbon. At that point, you can release the Alt key and start typing the hot key letters (by the way, you type all lowercase hot key letters — I only put them in caps to make them stand out in the text).

Hot key combos that use the Ctrl key are of an older vintage and work a little bit differently. On physical keyboards you have to hold down the Ctrl key while you type the hot key letter (though again, type only lowercase letters unless you see the Shift key in the sequence, as in Ctrl+Shift+C).

Excel 2013 uses only one pull-down menu (File) and one toolbar (the Quick Access toolbar). You open the File pull-down menu by clicking the File button or pressing Alt+F to access the Excel Backstage view. The Quick Access toolbar with its four buttons appears directly above the File button.

Finally, if you're really observant, you may notice a discrepancy in how the names of dialog box options (such as headings, option buttons, and check boxes) appear in the text and how they actually appear in Excel on your computer screen. I intentionally use the convention of capitalizing the initial letters of all the main words of a dialog box option to help you differentiate the name of the option from the rest of the text describing its use.

Icons Used in This Book

The following icons are placed in the margins to point out stuff you may or may not want to read.

This icon alerts you to nerdy discussions that you may well want to skip (or read when no one else is around).

This icon denotes a tidbit only for Excel users who are running Excel 2013 on some sort of touchscreen device such as a Windows 8 tablet or smartphone.

This icon alerts you to shortcuts or other valuable hints related to the topic at hand.

This icon alerts you to information to keep in mind if you want to meet with a modicum of success.

This icon alerts you to information to keep in mind if you want to avert complete disaster.

Where to Go from Here

If you've never worked with a computer spreadsheet, I suggest that you first go to Chapter 1 and find out what you're dealing with. Then, as specific needs arise (such as, "How do I copy a formula?" or "How do I print just a particular section of my worksheet?"), you can go to the Table of Contents or the index to find the appropriate section and go right to that section for answers.

Occasionally, John Wiley & Sons, Inc., has updates to its technology books. If this book has technical updates, they will be posted at www.dummies.com/go/excel2013updates.

Chapter 1

The Excel 2013 User Experience

- -

- -

*E*xcel 2013, like Excel 2010 and Excel 2007 before it, relies upon a single strip at the top of the worksheet called the Ribbon that puts the bulk of the Excel commands you use at your fingertips at all times.

Add to the Ribbon a File tab and a Quick Access toolbar — along with a few remaining task panes (Clipboard, Clip Art, and Research) — and you end up with the handiest way to crunch your numbers, produce and print polished financial reports, as well as organize and chart your data. In other words, to do all the wonderful things for which you rely on Excel.

Best of all, the Excel 2013 user interface includes all sorts of graphical elements that make working on spreadsheets a lot faster and a great deal easier. Foremost is Live Preview that shows you how your actual worksheet data would appear in a particular font, table formatting, and so on before you actually select it. This Live Preview extends to the new Quick Analysis and Recommended PivotTables and Recommended Charts commands to enable you to preview your data in various formats before you apply them.

Additionally, Excel 2013 supports a Page Layout View that displays rulers and margins along with headers and footers for every worksheet with a Zoom slider at the bottom of the screen that enables you to zoom in and out on the spreadsheet data instantly. Finally, Excel 2013 is full of pop-up galleries that make spreadsheet formatting and charting a real breeze, especially in tandem with Live Preview.

Excel's Ribbon User Interface

When you launch Excel 2013, the Start screen similar to the one shown in Figure 1-1 opens. Here you can start a new blank workbook by clicking the Blank workbook template, or you can select any of the other templates shown as the basis for your new spreadsheet. If none of the templates shown in the Start screen suits your needs, you can search for templates online. After you've worked with Excel for some time, the Start screen also displays a list of recently opened workbooks that you can reopen for further editing or printing.

Figure 1-1: The Excel 2013 Start screen enables you to open a new blank workbook, a recently opened workbook, or find a template to use as the basis for a new workbook.

When you select the Blank workbook template from the Excel 2013 Start screen, the program opens an initial worksheet (named Sheet1) in a new workbook file (named Book1) inside a program window like the one shown in Figure 1-2.

Quick Access toolbar   Ribbon

File button   Formula bar   Worksheet area   Unpin the Ribbon

Status bar

Figure 1-2: The Excel 2013 program window appears immediately after selecting the Blank Workbook template in the opening screen.

The Excel program window containing this worksheet of the workbook contains the following components:

✔ **File** button that when clicked opens the Backstage view — a menu on the left that contains all the document- and file-related commands, including Info, New, Open (selected by default when you first launch Excel), Save, Save As, Print, Share, Export, and Close. Additionally, at the bottom, there's an Account option with User and Product information and an Options item that enables you to change many of Excel's default settings. Note that you can exit the Backstage view and return to the normal worksheet view.

✔ Customizable **Quick Access toolbar** that contains buttons you can click to perform common tasks, such as saving your work and undoing and redoing edits. This toolbar is preceded by an **Excel program** button (sporting the Excel 2013 icon) with a drop-down menu of options that enable you to control the size and position of the Excel window and even close (exit) the program.

✔ **Ribbon** that contains the bulk of the Excel commands arranged into a series of tabs ranging from Home through View.

✔ **Formula bar** that displays the address of the current cell along with the contents of that cell.

✔ **Worksheet area** that contains the cells of the worksheet identified by column headings using letters along the top and row headings using numbers along the left edge; tabs for selecting new worksheets; a horizontal scroll bar to move left and right through the sheet; and a vertical scroll bar to move up and down through the sheet.

✔ **Status bar** that keeps you informed of the program's current mode and any special keys you engage and enables you to select a new worksheet view and to zoom in and out on the worksheet.

Going Backstage

To the immediate left of the Home tab on the Ribbon right below the Quick Access toolbar, you find the File button.

When you select File, the Backstage view opens. This view contains a menu similar to the one shown in Figure 1-3. When you open the Backstage view with the Info option selected, Excel displays at-a-glance stats about the workbook file you have open and active in the program.

Figure 1-3: Open Backstage view to get at-a-glance information about the current file, access all file-related commands, and modify the program options.

This information panel is divided into two panes. The pane on the left contains large buttons that enable you to modify the workbook's protection status, check the document before publishing, and manage its versions. The pane on the right contains a list of fields detailing the workbook's various Document Properties, some of which you can change (such as Title, Tags, Categories, Author, and Last Modified By), and many of which you can't (such as Size, Last Modified, Created, and so forth).

Below the Info option, you find the commands (New, Open, Save, Save As, Print, Share, Export, and Close) you commonly need for working with Excel workbook files. Near the bottom, the File tab contains an Account option that, when selected, displays an Account panel in the Backstage view. This panel displays user, connection, and Microsoft Office account information. Below the Account menu item, you find options that you can select to change the program's settings.

Select the Open option to open an Excel workbook you've worked on of late for more editing. When you select Open, Excel displays a panel with a list of all the workbook files recently opened in the program. To re-open a particular file for editing, all you do is click its filename in this list.

To close the Backstage view and return to the normal worksheet view, select the Back button at the very top of the menu or simply press Esc on your keyboard.

Using the Excel Ribbon

The Ribbon (shown in Figure 1-4) groups the most commonly used options needed to perform particular types of Excel tasks.

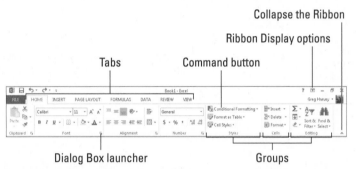

Figure 1-4: Excel's Ribbon consists of a series of tabs containing command buttons arranged into different groups.

To do this, the Ribbon uses the following components:

- ✔ **Tabs** for each of Excel's main tasks that bring together and display all the commands commonly needed to perform that core task.

- ✔ **Groups** that organize related command buttons into subtasks normally performed as part of the tab's larger core task.

- ✔ **Command buttons** within each group that you select to perform a particular action or to open a gallery from which you can click a particular thumbnail. *Note:* Many command buttons on certain tabs of the Ribbon are organized into mini-toolbars with related settings.

✔ **Dialog Box launcher** in the lower-right corner of certain groups that opens a dialog box containing a bunch of additional options you can select.

To display more of the Worksheet area in the program window, collapse the Ribbon so that only its tabs are displayed by simply clicking the Collapse the Ribbon button on the right side above the vertical scroll bar. You can also double-click (or double-tap on a touchscreen) any one of the Ribbon's tabs, or press Ctrl+F1 on your keyboard. To once again pin the Ribbon in place so that all the command buttons on each of its tabs are always displayed in the program window, double-click (or double-tap) any one of the tabs, or press Ctrl+F1 a second time. You can also do this by selecting the Pin the Ribbon button (whose icon looks just like a pin) that replaces the Unpin the Ribbon button and appears whenever you temporarily activate a tab to use its command buttons.

When you work in Excel with the Ribbon collapsed, the Ribbon expands each time you activate one of its tabs to show its command buttons, but that tab stays open only until you select one of the command buttons or select an element in the worksheet. The moment you select a command button, Excel immediately minimizes the Ribbon again and just displays its tabs. Note that you can also use the Show Tabs and Show Tabs and Commands options on the Ribbon Display Options button's drop-down menu to switch between collapsing the Ribbon to its tabs and restoring its commands again.

Keeping tabs on the Ribbon

The first time you launch a new workbook in Excel 2013, its Ribbon contains the following tabs from left to right:

✔ **Home** tab with the command buttons normally used when creating, formatting, and editing a spreadsheet, arranged into the Clipboard, Font, Alignment, Number, Styles, Cells, and Editing groups.

✔ **Insert** tab with the command buttons normally used when adding particular elements (including graphics, PivotTables, charts, hyperlinks, and headers and footers) to a spreadsheet, arranged into the Tables, Illustrations, Apps, Charts, Reports, Sparklines, Filter, Links, Text, and Symbols groups.

✔ **Page Layout** tab with the command buttons normally used when preparing a spreadsheet for printing or re-ordering graphics on the sheet, arranged into the Themes, Page Setup, Scale to Fit, Sheet Options, and Arrange groups.

✔ **Formulas** tab with the command buttons normally used when adding formulas and functions to a spreadsheet or checking a worksheet for formula errors, arranged into the Function Library, Defined Names, Formula Auditing, and Calculation groups. *Note:* This tab also contains a Solutions group when you activate certain add-in programs, such as Analysis ToolPak and Euro Currency Tools. See Chapter 4 for more on using Excel add-in programs.

✔ **Data** tab with the command buttons normally used when importing, querying, outlining, and subtotaling the data placed into a worksheet's data list, arranged into the Get External Data, Connections, Sort & Filter, Data Tools, and Outline groups. *Note:* This tab also contains an Analysis group when you activate add-ins, such as Analysis ToolPak and Solver. See Chapter 4 for more on Excel add-ins.

✔ **Review** tab with the command buttons normally used when proofing, protecting, and marking up a spreadsheet for review by others, arranged into the Proofing, Language, Comments, and Changes groups. *Note:* This tab also contains an Ink group with a sole Start Inking button when you're running Office 2013 on a device with a touchscreen such as a Tablet PC or a computer equipped with a digital ink tablet.

✔ **View** tab with the command buttons normally used when changing the display of the Worksheet area and the data it contains, arranged into the Workbook Views, Show, Zoom, Window, and Macros groups.

In addition to these standard seven tabs, Excel has an eighth, optional Developer tab that you can add to the Ribbon if you do a lot of work with macros and XML files. See Chapter 4 for more on the Developer tab. If you are running a version of Excel 2013 with the PowerPivot add-in installed, a PowerPivot tab appears near the end of the Ribbon.

Although these standard tabs are the ones you always see on the Ribbon when it's displayed in Excel, they aren't the only things that can appear in this area. Excel can display contextual tools when you're working with a particular object that you select in the worksheet, such as a graphic image you've added or a chart or PivotTable you've created. The name of the contextual tool for the selected object appears immediately above the tab or tabs associated with the tools.

For example, Figure 1-5 shows a worksheet after you click the embedded chart to select it. As you can see, this adds the contextual tool called Chart Tools to the very end of the Ribbon. The Chart Tools contextual tool has two tabs: Design (selected) and Format. Note, too, that the command buttons on the Design tab are arranged into the groups Chart Layouts, Chart Styles, Data, Type, and Location.

Chart Tools contextual tab

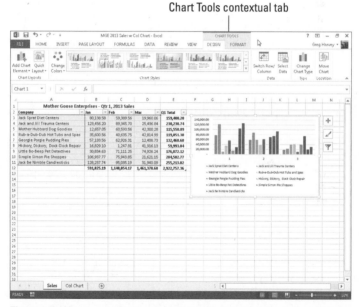

Figure 1-5: When you select certain objects in the worksheet, Excel adds contextual tools to the Ribbon with their own tabs, groups, and command buttons.

The moment you deselect the object (usually by clicking somewhere outside the object's boundaries), the contextual tool for that object and all its tabs immediately disappear from the Ribbon, leaving only the regular tabs — Home, Insert, Page Layout, Formulas, Data, Review, and View — displayed.

Selecting commands with mouse and keyboard

Because Excel 2013 runs on many different types of devices, the most efficient means of selecting Ribbon commands depends not only on the device on which you're running the program, but also on the way that device is equipped.

For example, when I run Excel 2013 on my Windows 8 tablet in its dock equipped with a physical keyboard and with my optical wireless mouse connected, I select commands from the Excel Ribbon more or less the same way I do when running Excel on my Windows desktop computer equipped with a stand-alone physical keyboard and mouse or laptop computer with its built-in physical keyboard and trackpad.

However, when I run Excel 2013 on my Windows 8 tablet without access to the dock with its physical keyboard and mouse, I am limited to selecting Ribbon commands directly on the touchscreen with my finger or stylus.

The most direct method for selecting Ribbon commands equipped with a physical keyboard and mouse is to click the tab that contains the command button you want and then click that button in its group. For example, to insert an online image into your spreadsheet, you click the Insert tab and then click the Illustrations button followed by the Online Pictures button to open the Insert Pictures dialog box.

The easiest method for selecting commands on the Ribbon — if you know your keyboard at all well — is to press the keyboard's Alt key and then type the letter of the hot key that appears on the tab you want to select. Excel then displays all the command button hot keys next to their buttons, along with the hot keys for the dialog box launchers in any group on that tab. To select a command button or dialog box launcher, simply type its hot key letter.

If you know the old Excel shortcut keys from versions prior to Excel 2007, you can still use them. For example, instead of going through the rigmarole of pressing Alt+HCC to copy a cell selection to the Windows Clipboard and then Alt+HVP to paste it elsewhere in the sheet, you can still press Ctrl+C to copy the selection and then press Ctrl+V when you're ready to paste it.

Selecting commands by touch

Before trying to select Excel Ribbon commands by touch, however, you definitely want to turn on Touch mode in Excel 2013. When you do this, Excel spreads out the command buttons on the Ribbon tabs by putting more space around them, making it more likely you'll actually select the command button you're tapping with your finger (or even a more slender stylus) instead of one right next to it. (This is a particular problem with the command buttons in the Font group on the Home tab that enable you to add different attributes to cell entries such as bold, italic, or underlining: They are so close together when Touch mode is off that they are almost impossible to correctly select by touch.)

To do this, simply tap the Touch/Mouse Mode button that appears near the end of the Quick Access toolbar sandwiched between the Redo and Customize Quick Access Toolbar buttons. When you tap this button a drop-down menu with two options, Mouse and Touch, appears. Tap the Touch option to put your touchscreen tablet or laptop into Touch mode.

Although the Touch/Mouse Mode button is automatically added to the Excel 2013 Quick Access toolbar only when running the program on a tablet or personal computer equipped with a touchscreen, that doesn't mean you can't use it to switch between Touch mode (with more space between Ribbon command buttons) and Mouse mode on a standard computer without touchscreen technology. All you have to do is add the Touch/Mouse Mode button to the Quick Access toolbar (see "Customizing the Quick Access toolbar" that follows for details).

Customizing the Quick Access toolbar

When you start using Excel 2013, the Quick Access toolbar contains only the following few buttons:

- ✔ **Save** to save any changes made to the current workbook using the same filename, file format, and location

- ✔ **Undo** to undo the last editing, formatting, or layout change you made

✔ **Redo** to reapply the previous editing, formatting, or layout change that you just removed with the Undo button

✔ **Touch/Mouse Mode** (tablets and computers with touch-screens only) to place more space around Ribbon command buttons to make it easier to select commands with your finger or stylus

The Quick Access toolbar is very customizable because Excel makes it easy to add any Ribbon command to it. Moreover, you're not restricted to adding buttons for just the commands on the Ribbon; you can add any Excel command you want to the toolbar, even the obscure ones that don't rate an appearance on any of its tabs.

By default, the Quick Access toolbar appears above the Ribbon tabs immediately to the right of the Excel program button (used to resize the workbook window or quit the program). To display the toolbar beneath the Ribbon immediately above the Formula bar, click the Customize Quick Access Toolbar button (the drop-down button to the right of the toolbar with a horizontal bar above a down-pointing triangle) and then click Show Below the Ribbon on its drop-down menu. You will definitely want to make this change if you start adding more than just a few extra buttons to the toolbar. That way, the growing Quick Access toolbar doesn't start crowding the name of the current workbook that appears to the toolbar's right.

Adding Customize Quick Access Toolbar's menu commands

When you click the Customize Quick Access Toolbar button, a drop-down menu appears containing the following commands:

✔ **New** to open a new workbook

✔ **Open** to display the Open dialog box for opening an existing workbook

✔ **Save** to save changes to your current workbook

✔ **Email** to open your mail

✔ **Quick Print** to send the current worksheet to your default printer

✔ **Print Preview and Print** to open the Print panel in Backstage view with a preview of the current worksheet in the right pane

- ✔ **Spelling** to check the current worksheet for spelling errors

- ✔ **Undo** to undo your latest worksheet edit

- ✔ **Redo** to reapply the last edit that you removed with Undo

- ✔ **Sort Ascending** to sort the current cell selection or column in A to Z alphabetical order, lowest to highest numerical order, or oldest to newest date order

- ✔ **Sort Descending** to sort the current cell selection or column in Z to A alphabetical order, highest to lowest numerical order, or newest to oldest date order

- ✔ **Touch /Mouse Mode** to switch in and out of Touch mode that adds extra space around the command buttons on the individual Ribbon tabs to make them easier to select on a touchscreen device regardless of whether you tap with your finger or a stylus

When you open this menu, only the Save, Undo, and Redo options are the ones selected (indicated by the check marks); therefore, these buttons are the only buttons to appear on the Quick Access toolbar. To add any of the other commands on this menu to the toolbar, simply click the option on the drop-down menu. Excel then adds a button for that command to the end of the Quick Access toolbar (and a check mark to its option on the drop-down menu).

To remove a command button that you add to the Quick Access toolbar in this manner, click the option a second time on the Customize Quick Access Toolbar button's drop-down menu. Excel removes its command button from the toolbar and the check mark from its option on the drop-down menu.

Adding Ribbon commands

To add a Ribbon command to the Quick Access toolbar, open the command button's shortcut menu (right-click with a mouse or tap and hold on a touchscreen) and then select the Add to Quick Access Toolbar menu item. Excel then immediately adds the selected Ribbon command button to the very end of the Quick Access toolbar, immediately in front of the Customize Quick Access Toolbar button.

If you want to move the command button to a new location on the Quick Access toolbar or group it with other buttons on the toolbar, select the Customize Quick Access Toolbar button followed by the More Commands option near the bottom of its drop-down menu.

Excel then opens the Excel Options dialog box with the Quick Access Toolbar tab selected (similar to the one shown in Figure 1-6). On the right side of the dialog box, Excel shows all the buttons added to the Quick Access toolbar. The order in which they appear from left to right on the toolbar corresponds to the top-down order in the list box.

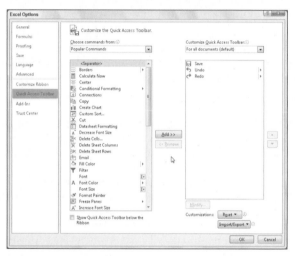

Figure 1-6: Use the buttons on the Quick Access Toolbar tab of the Excel Options dialog box to customize the appearance of the Quick Access toolbar.

To reposition a particular button on the toolbar, select it in the list box on the right and then select either the Move Up button (the one with the black triangle pointing upward) or the Move Down button (the one with the black triangle pointing downward) until the button is promoted or demoted to the desired position on the toolbar.

You can add a pair of vertical separators to the toolbar to group related buttons. To do this, select the <Separator> option in the list box on the left followed by the Add button twice. Then, select the Move Up or Move Down button to position one of the two separators at the beginning of the group and the other at the end.

To remove a button you've added, open the Quick Access toolbar's shortcut menu (right-click or tap and hold on a touchscreen) and then select the Remove from Quick Access Toolbar option.

Adding non-Ribbon commands to the Quick Access toolbar

You can also use the options on the Quick Access Toolbar tab of the Excel Options dialog box (refer to Figure 1-6) to add a button for any Excel command even if it isn't one of those displayed on the tabs of the Ribbon:

1. **Select the type of command you want to add to the Quick Access toolbar in the Choose Commands From drop-down list box.**

   The types of commands include the Popular Commands pull-down menu (the default) as well as each of the tabs that appear on the Ribbon. To display only the commands that are not displayed on the Ribbon, select Commands Not in the Ribbon near the top of the drop-down list. To display a complete list of the Excel commands, select All Commands near the top of the drop-down list.

2. **Select the command button you want to add to the Quick Access toolbar in the list box on the left.**

3. **Click the Add button to add the command button to the bottom of the list box on the right.**

4. **(Optional) To reposition the newly added command button so that it isn't the last one on the toolbar, click the Move Up button until it's in the desired position.**

5. **Click OK to close the Excel Options dialog box.**

If you've created favorite macros (see Chapter 4) that you routinely use and want to be able to run directly from the Quick Access toolbar, select Macros in the Choose Commands From drop-down list box in the Excel Options dialog box and then click the name of the macro to add followed by the Add button.

Having fun with the Formula bar

The Formula bar displays the cell address (determined by a column letter(s) followed by a row number) and the contents of the current cell. For example, cell A1 is the first cell of each worksheet at the intersection of column A and row 1; cell XFD1048576 is the last cell of each worksheet at the intersection of column XFD and row 1048576. The type of entry you make determines the contents of the current cell: text or numbers, for example, if you enter a heading or particular value, or the details of a formula, if you enter a calculation.

The Formula bar has three sections:

✔ **Name box:** The left-most section that displays the address of the current cell address.

✔ **Formula bar buttons:** The second, middle section that appears as a rather nondescript button displaying only an indented circle on the left (used to narrow or widen the Name box) and the Insert Function button (labeled *fx*) on the right. When you start making or editing a cell entry, Cancel (an *X*) and Enter (a check mark) buttons appear between them.

✔ **Cell contents:** The third, right-most white area to the immediate right of the Insert Function button takes up the rest of the bar and expands as necessary to display really long cell entries that won't fit in the normal area.

The cell contents section of the Formula bar is important because it *always* shows you the contents of the cell even when the worksheet does not. (When you're dealing with a formula, Excel displays only the calculated result in the cell in the worksheet and not the formula by which that result is derived.) Additionally, you can edit the contents of the cell in this area at any time. Similarly, when the cell contents area is blank, you know that the cell is empty as well.

What to do in the Worksheet area

The Worksheet area is where most of the Excel spreadsheet action takes place because it's the place that displays the cells in different sections of the current worksheet and it's right inside the cells that you do all your spreadsheet data entry and formatting, not to mention a great deal of your editing.

To enter or edit data in a cell, that cell must be current. Excel indicates that a cell is current in three ways:

- ✔ The cell cursor — the dark green border surrounding the cell's entire perimeter — appears in the cell.

- ✔ The address of the cell appears in the Name box of the Formula bar.

- ✔ The cell's column letter(s) and row number are shaded in the column headings and row headings that appear at the top and left of the Worksheet area, respectively.

Moving around the worksheet

An Excel worksheet contains far too many columns and rows for all a worksheet's cells to be displayed at one time, regardless of how large your computer's monitor screen is or how high the screen resolution. (After all, we're talking 17,179,869,184 cells total!) Therefore, Excel offers many methods for moving the cell cursor around the worksheet to the cell where you want to enter new data or edit existing data:

- ✔ Click the desired cell — assuming that the cell is displayed within the section of the sheet visible in the Worksheet area — either by clicking it with your mouse or tapping it on your touchscreen.

  Click the Name box, then type the address of the desired cell and press the Enter key.

- ✔ Press F5 to open the Go To dialog box, type the address of the desired cell into its Reference text box, and then click OK.

- ✔ Use the cursor keys, as shown in Table 1-1 to move the cell cursor to the desired cell.

- ✔ Use the horizontal and vertical buttons located at the ends of the scroll bars found at the bottom and right edge of the Worksheet area to move to the part of the worksheet that contains the desired cell and then click or tap the cell to put the cell cursor in it.

Keystroke shortcuts for moving the cell cursor

Excel offers a wide variety of keystrokes for moving the cell cursor to a new cell. When you use one of these keystrokes, the program automatically scrolls a new part of the worksheet into view, if this is required to move the cell pointer. In Table 1-1, I summarize these keystrokes, including how far each one moves the cell pointer from its starting position.

Table 1-1 Keystrokes for Moving the Cell Cursor

Keystroke	Where the Cell Cursor Moves
→ or Tab	Cell to the immediate right.
← or Shift+Tab	Cell to the immediate left.
↑	Cell up one row.
↓	Cell down one row.
Home	Cell in Column A of the current row.
Ctrl+Home	First cell (A1) of the worksheet.
Ctrl+End or End, Home	Cell in the worksheet at the intersection of the last column that has data in it and the last row that has data in it (that is, the last cell of the so-called active area of the worksheet).
Page Up	Cell one full screen up in the same column.
Page Down	Cell one full screen down in the same column.
Ctrl+→ or End, →	First occupied cell to the right in the same row that is either preceded or followed by a blank cell. If no cell is occupied, the pointer goes to the cell at the very end of the row.
Ctrl+← or End, ←	First occupied cell to the left in the same row that is either preceded or followed by a blank cell. If no cell is occupied, the pointer goes to the cell at the very beginning of the row.
Ctrl+↑ or End, ↑	First occupied cell above in the same column that is either preceded or followed by a blank cell. If no cell is occupied, the pointer goes to the cell at the very top of the column.
Ctrl+↓ or End, ↓	First occupied cell below in the same column that is either preceded or followed by a blank cell. If no cell is occupied, the pointer goes to the cell at the very bottom of the column.
Ctrl+Page Down	The cell pointer's location in the next worksheet of that workbook.
Ctrl+Page Up	The cell pointer's location in the previous worksheet of that workbook.

Note: *In the case of those keystrokes that use arrow keys, you must either use the arrows on the cursor keypad or else have the Num Lock disengaged on the numeric keypad of your keyboard.*

The keystrokes that combine the Ctrl or End key with an arrow key listed in Table 1-1 are among the most helpful for moving quickly from one edge to the other in large tables of cell entries or for moving from table to table in a section of a worksheet with many blocks of cells.

When you use Ctrl and an arrow key to move from edge to edge in a table or between tables in a worksheet, you hold down Ctrl while you press one of the four arrow keys (indicated by the + symbol in keystrokes, such as Ctrl+→).

When you use End and an arrow-key alternative, you must press and then release the End key *before* you press the arrow key (indicated by the comma in keystrokes, such as End, →). Pressing and releasing the End key causes the End Mode indicator to appear on the Status bar. This is your sign that Excel is ready for you to press one of the four arrow keys.

Because you can keep the Ctrl key depressed while you press the different arrow keys that you need to use, the Ctrl-plus-arrow-key method provides a more fluid method for navigating blocks of cells than the End-then-arrow-key method.

You can use the Scroll Lock key to "freeze" the position of the cell pointer in the worksheet so that you can scroll new areas of the worksheet in view with keystrokes, such as PgUp (Page Up) and PgDn (Page Down), without changing the cell pointer's original position (in essence, making these keystrokes work in the same manner as the scroll bars).

After engaging Scroll Lock, when you scroll the worksheet with the keyboard, Excel does not select a new cell while it brings a new section of the worksheet into view. To "unfreeze" the cell pointer when scrolling the worksheet via the keyboard, you just press the Scroll Lock key again.

Tips on using the Touch keyboard

If you're running Excel 2013 on a device that lacks any kind of physical keyboard, you need to open the Touch keyboard and use it to input your spreadsheet data.

To open the Touch keyboard, simply tap the Touch Keyboard button that appears on the right side of the Windows 7 or 8 taskbar. Doing this displays the Touch keyboard, floating undocked at the bottom of the Excel program window.

To dock the Touch keyboard beneath the Excel 2013 program window, simply click the Dock button that appears to the immediate left of the Close button in the upper-right corner of the keyboard. Figure 1-7 shows how your touchscreen looks after docking the Windows 8 Touch keyboard.

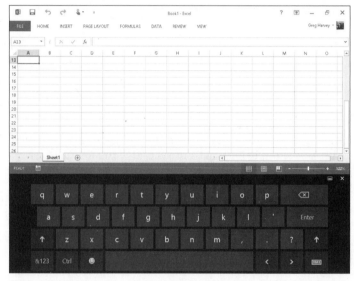

Figure 1-7: Windows 8 touchscreen shown after displaying and docking the Touch keyboard beneath the Excel 2013 program window.

As shown in this figure, when docked, the Windows 8 Touch keyboard remains completely separate from the Excel program window so that you still have access to all the cells in the current worksheet when doing your data entry. The Windows 8 Touch keyboard is limited mostly to letter keys above a space-bar with a few punctuation symbols (apostrophe, comma, period, and question mark). This keyboard also sports the following special keys:

- ✔ **Backspace** key (marked with the x in the shape pointing left) to delete characters to the immediate left when entering or editing a cell entry

- ✔ **Enter** key to complete an entry in the current cell and move the cursor down one row in the same column

- ✔ **Shift** keys (with an arrow pointing upward) to enter capital letters in a cell entry

- ✔ **Numeric** key (with the &123) to switch to the Touch keyboard so that it displays a numeric keyboard with a Tab key and extensive punctuation used in entering numeric data in a cell (tap the &123 key a second time to return to the standard QWERTY letter arrangement)

- ✔ **Ctrl** key to run macros to which you've assigned letter keys (see Chapter 4 for details) or to combine with the Left arrow or Right arrow key to jump the cursor to the cell in the last and first column of the current row, respectively

- ✔ **Emoticon** key (with that awful smiley face icon) to switch to emoticons that you can enter into a cell entry (tap the Emoticon key a second time to return to standard QWERTY letter arrangement)

- ✔ **Left** arrow (with the < symbol) to move the cell cursor one cell to the immediate right and complete any cell entry in progress

- ✔ **Right** arrow (with the > symbol) to move the cell cursor one cell to the immediate left and complete any cell entry in progress

When you finish entering your worksheet data with the Windows 8 Touch keyboard, you can close it and return to the normal full screen view of the Excel program window by tapping the Close button.

The Windows 8 Touch keyboard supports a split-keyboard arrangement that separates the QWERTY letter keys into two banks on the left and right with a ten-key numeric keypad in the middle. The drawback is that the individual keys are smaller than the normal, non-split arrangement and can be harder to select with your finger or stylus. The big bonus is that you can enter both numbers and text into the cells of your worksheet without having to switch back and forth between the QWERTY letter and numeric key arrangements. To switch to the split-keyboard arrangement, tap the Keyboard button in the very lower-right corner of the Touch keyboard (to the immediate right of the Right arrow key) and then tap second button from the left (that shows a gap in the keyboard icon) in the pop-up menu that appears.

Tips on using the scroll bars

To understand how scrolling works in Excel, imagine its humongous worksheet as a papyrus scroll attached to rollers on the left and right. To bring into view a section of papyrus hidden on the right, crank the left roller until the section with the cells that you want to see appears. Likewise, to scroll into view a worksheet section hidden on the left, crank the right roller until the section of cells appears.

You can use the horizontal scroll bar at the bottom of the Worksheet area to scroll back and forth through the columns of a worksheet and the vertical scroll bar to scroll up and down through its rows. To scroll a column or a row at a time in a particular direction, select the appropriate scroll arrow at the ends of the scroll bar. To jump immediately back to the originally displayed area of the worksheet after scrolling through single columns or rows in this fashion, simply click (tap on a touchscreen) the area in the scroll bar that now appears in front of or after the scroll bar.

You can resize the horizontal scroll bar making it wider or narrower by dragging the button that appears to the immediate left of its left scroll arrow. Just keep in mind when working in a workbook that contains a whole bunch of worksheets that widening the horizontal scroll bar can hide the display of the workbook's later sheet tabs.

 To scroll very quickly through columns or rows of the worksheet when you have a physical keyboard available, hold down the Shift key and then drag the scroll button in the appropriate direction within the scroll bar until the columns or rows that you want to see appear on the screen in the Worksheet area. When you hold down the Shift key while you scroll, the scroll button within the scroll bar becomes skinny and a ScreenTip appears next to the scroll bar, keeping you informed of the letter(s) of the columns or the numbers of the rows that you're whizzing through.

If you have a mouse and it's equipped with a wheel, you can use it to scroll directly through the columns and rows of the worksheet without using the horizontal or vertical scroll bars. Simply position the white cross mouse pointer in the center of the Worksheet area and then hold down the wheel button of the mouse. When the mouse pointer changes to a four-pointed arrow with a black dot in its center, drag the mouse pointer in the appropriate direction (left and right to scroll through columns or up and down to scroll through rows) until the desired column or row comes into view in the Worksheet area.

On a touchscreen device, you can also scroll new parts of a worksheet into view simply by swiping with your finger or stylus to scroll (by dragging it on the screen). To scroll new worksheet columns on the right into view, swipe right-to-left. To scroll new worksheet rows from below into view, swipe up, bottom to top. The force with which you slide determines how many columns or rows you scroll through. To return previously displayed columns or rows into view, simply slide in the opposite direction: left to right to scroll columns left and downward to scroll rows up.

The only disadvantage to using the scroll bars to move around is that the scroll bars bring only new sections of the worksheet into view — they don't actually change the position of the cell cursor. If you want to start making entries in the cells in a new area of the worksheet, you still have to remember to select the cell (by clicking it) or the group of cells (by dragging through them) where you want the data to appear before you begin entering the data.

Surfing the sheets in a workbook

Each new workbook you open in Excel 2013 contains a single blank worksheet with 16,384 columns and 1,048,576 rows (giving you a truly staggering 17,179,869,184 blank cells!). But, that's not all. If ever you need more worksheets in your workbook, you can add them simply by clicking the New Sheet button (indicated by the plus sign in a circle) that appears to the immediate right of the last visible tab (see callout in Figure 1-8) or by selecting Shift+F11.

Previous sheet   Sheet tabs   New sheet

Tab Scroll buttons   Next sheet

Figure 1-8: The Sheet Tab scroll buttons, sheet tabs, Next sheet, Previous sheet, and New Sheet buttons enable you to activate your worksheets and add to them.

On the left side of the bottom of the Worksheet area, the Sheet Tab scroll buttons appear followed by the actual tabs for the worksheets in your workbook and the New Sheet button. To activate a worksheet for editing, select it by clicking its sheet tab. Excel lets you know what sheet is active by displaying the sheet name in boldface type and underlining it to make its tab appear connected to the current sheet.

Don't forget the Ctrl+Page Down and Ctrl+Page Up shortcut keys for selecting the next and previous sheet, respectively, in your workbook.

If your workbook contains too many sheets for all the tabs to be displayed at the bottom of the Worksheet area, use the Sheet Tab scroll buttons to bring new tabs into view (so that you can then click them to activate them). You click the Next Sheet button (the ellipsis or three periods to the left of the first visible sheet) to scroll the next hidden sheet tab into view or the Last Sheet button (the ellipsis or three periods to the left of the last visible sheet) to scroll the last group of completely or partially hidden tabs into view.

To scroll the very first worksheet in the workbook into view, you can hold down Ctrl as you click the left-pointing Sheet Tab scroll button. To scroll the last sheet into view, Ctrl+click the right-pointing scroll button.

To display the Activate dialog box that lists all the sheets in the workbook from first to last, right-click either one of the Sheet Tab scroll buttons. You can then scroll into view and click any of the sheets in the workbook simply by clicking its name in the Activate dialog followed by clicking OK.

On a touchscreen device, remember that the touch equivalent of a right-click with a mouse is to tap and press the graphic element on the screen — the Sheet Tab scroll button in this case — until a circle appears around your finger or stylus. When you then remove your finger or stylus from the screen, the shortcut menu or, in this case, the dialog box associated with the graphic element appears.

Showing off the Status bar

The Status bar is the last component at the very bottom of the Excel program window (see Figure 1-9). The Status bar contains the following:

- ✔ **Mode indicator** on the left that shows the current state of the Excel program (Ready, Edit, and so on) as well as any special keys that are engaged (Caps Lock, Num Lock, and Scroll Lock).

- ✔ **AutoCalculate indicator** that displays the average and sum of all the numerical entries in the current cell selection along with the count of every cell in the selection.

- ✔ **Layout selector** that enables you to select between three layouts for the Worksheet area: Normal, the default view that shows only the worksheet cells with the column and row headings; Page Layout View that adds rulers, page margins, and shows page breaks for the worksheet; and Page Break Preview that enables you to adjust the paging of a report. (See Chapter 5 for details.)

- ✔ **Zoom slider** that enables you to zoom in and out on the cells in the Worksheet area by dragging the slider to the right or left, respectively.

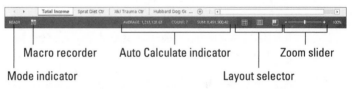

Macro recorder   Auto Calculate indicator   Zoom slider

Mode indicator   Layout selector

Figure 1-9: The Status bar displays the program's current standing and enables you to select new worksheet views.

On a touchscreen device, you can work the Zoom slider by using the Pinch and Stretch gesture to increase and decrease the size of the cells displayed in your worksheet. As you stretch your thumb and forefinger apart, you zoom in on the worksheet and the Zoom slider moves to the right and the percentage increases. As you pinch your fingers together, you zoom out on the worksheet and the Zoom slider moves to the left and the percentage decreases.

The Num Lock indicator on a physical keyboard equipped with a numeric keypad tells you that you can use the keypad to enter values in the worksheet. This keypad will most often be separate from the regular keyboard (on the right side if you're using a separate keyboard) and embedded in keys on the right side of the keyboard on almost all laptop computers where the keyboard is built in to the computer.

Launching and Quitting Excel

Excel 2013 runs only under Windows 7 and the new Windows 8 operating system. This means that if your PC is running the old Vista or XP versions of Windows, you must upgrade before you can successfully install and run Excel 2013. Because of the significant changes made to the user interface in Windows 8, the procedure for starting Excel 2013 on this operating system is quite a bit different from Windows 7.

Starting Excel from the Windows 8 Start screen

When starting Excel 2013 from the Windows 8 Start screen, simply select the Excel 2013 program tile either by clicking it if you have a mouse available or tapping it with your finger or stylus if you're running Windows 8 on a touchscreen device.

If you can't locate the Excel 2013 tile among those displayed on the Start screen, use the Search feature to find the application and pin it to the Windows 8 Start screen:

1. **From the Start screen, begin typing** exc **on your physical or virtual keyboard.**

   Windows 8 displays Excel 2013 in the list of programs under Apps on the left side of the screen.

2. **Right-click the Excel 2013 button in the Apps list on the left side of the screen.**

   On a touchscreen device, the equivalent to the right-click of the mouse is to tap and hold the Excel 2013 menu item until a circle appears around your finger or stylus. Then, when you remove the finger or stylus from the screen, the shortcut menu appears.

3. **Select the Pin to Start option in the menu bar that appears at the bottom of the screen.**

After pinning an Excel 2013 tile to the Windows 8 Start screen, you can move it by dragging and dropping it in your desired block.

Starting Excel from the Windows 7 Start menu

When starting Excel 2013 from the Windows 7 Start menu, follow these simple steps:

1. **Click the Start button on the Windows taskbar to open the Windows Start menu.**

   To select the Start button on a touchscreen device with no mouse, tap the button on the touchscreen.

2. **Select All Programs on the Start menu followed by the Microsoft Office 2013 and Excel 2013 options on the continuation menus.**

You can use the Search Programs and Files search box on the Windows 7 Start menu to locate Excel on your computer and launch the program in no time at all:

1. **Click the Start button on the Windows taskbar to open the Windows Start menu.**

2. **Click in the Start menu's search text box and type the letters** exc **to have Windows locate Microsoft Office Excel 2013 on your computer.**

   If you're using a device without a physical keyboard, double-tap the right edge of the virtual keyboard that appears on the left edge of the Windows Start menu and screen to make the entire keyboard appear and then tap out the letters **exc**.

3. **Select the Microsoft Excel 2013 option that now appears in the left Programs column on the Start menu.**

Adding an Excel 2013 shortcut to your Windows 7 desktop

Some people prefer having the Excel program icon appear on the Windows desktop so that they can launch the program from the desktop by double-clicking this program icon. To create an Excel 2013 program shortcut for your Windows 7 desktop, follow these simple steps:

1. **Click the Windows Start button and then select the All Programs option on the Start menu.**

   Windows 7 displays a new menu of program options on the Start menu.

2. **Select the Microsoft Office 2013 option on the Start menu.**

   Windows displays a submenu listing all the Office 2013 programs installed on your device.

3. **Drag the Excel 2013 item from the Start menu to the Windows 7 desktop and drop it in the desired position.**

   As you drag the icon to the desktop, the screen tip "Move to Desktop" appears under the outline of the icon. When you drop the icon in place on the desktop, Windows adds an Excel 2013 shortcut icon that launches the program when you double-click it with a mouse or double-tap it with your finger or a stylus on a touch-screen device.

Pinning Excel 2013 to your Windows 7 Start menu

If you use Excel all the time, you may want to make its program option a permanent part of the Windows 7 Start menu. To do this, pin the program option to the Start menu:

1. **Click the Windows Start button and then select the All Programs option on the Start menu.**

   Windows 7 displays a new menu of program options on their Start menus.

2. **Select the Microsoft Office 2013 option from the Start menu.**

   Windows 7 displays a submenu listing the Office 2013 programs.

3. **Right-click Excel 2013 on the Windows continuation or submenu to open its shortcut menu.**

   On a touchscreen device, the equivalent to the right-click of the mouse is to tap and hold the Excel 2013 menu item until a circle appears around your finger or stylus. Then, when you remove the finger or stylus from the screen, the shortcut menu appears.

4. Select Pin to Start Menu on the shortcut menu.

After pinning Excel in this manner, the Excel 2013 option always appears in the upper section of the left-hand column of the Windows Start menu, and you can then launch Excel simply by opening the Windows Start button and then selecting this menu option.

After you pin the Excel 2013 option onto the Windows 7 Start menu, Windows adds a continuation button to the right of the menu item. Whenever you highlight this menu item with a mouse (or tap it on a touchscreen), Windows 7 automatically expands the Start menu to display a list of your recently opened Excel workbook files. You can then open one of these files for further editing at the same time you launch the Excel 2013 program simply by selecting its filename on the continuation menu.

Pinning Excel 2013 to the Windows 7 taskbar

Instead of, or in addition to, pinning Excel 2013 to the Windows 7 Start menu, you can pin an Excel 2013 button to the Windows taskbar.

All you do is drag and drop the Excel 2013 icon that either you pinned to the Windows Start menu or you added as a shortcut to the Windows desktop into its desired position on the Windows 7 taskbar. (See "Pinning Excel 2013 to your Windows 7 Start menu" and "Adding an Excel 2013 shortcut to your Windows 7 desktop" earlier in this chapter for details.)

After pinning a Microsoft Excel 2013 icon to the Windows 7 taskbar, the button appears on the Windows taskbar each time you start your computer, and you can launch the Excel program simply by single-clicking its icon with your mouse or tapping it with your finger or stylus on a touchscreen device.

Exiting Excel

When you're ready to call it a day and quit Excel, you have a couple of choices for shutting down the program:

- ✔ Press Alt+F4 on your physical or virtual keyboard.
- ✔ Click or tap (on a touchscreen device) the Close button (the X) in the upper-right corner of the Excel program window.

If you try to exit Excel after working on a workbook and you haven't saved your latest changes, the program displays an alert box querying whether you want to save your changes. To save your changes before exiting, select the Save command button. (For detailed information on saving documents, see Chapter 2.) If you've just been playing around in the worksheet and don't want to save your changes, you can abandon the document by selecting the Don't Save button instead.

Help Is on the Way

You can get online help with Excel 2013 any time that you need it while using the program. Simply click the Help button (the button with the question mark icon to the immediate right of the Minimize the Ribbon button on the right side of the program window opposite the Ribbon's tabs) or press F1 to open a separate Excel Help window.

When the Excel Help window opens, Excel attempts to use your Internet connection to update its topics. The opening Excel Help window contains links that you can click to get information on what's new in the program.

To get help with a particular command or function, use the Search Help text box at the top of the Excel Help window. Type keywords or a phrase describing your topic (such as "print preview" or "printing worksheets") in this text box and then press Enter or click the Search button. The Excel Help window then presents a list of links to related help topics that you can click to display the information.

Chapter 2

Creating a Spreadsheet from Scratch

*A*fter you know how to launch Excel 2013, it's time to find out how not to get yourself into trouble when actually using it! In this chapter, you find out how to put all kinds of information into all those little, blank worksheet cells I describe in Chapter 1. Here you find out about the Excel AutoCorrect and AutoComplete features and how they can help cut down on errors and speed up your work. You also get some basic pointers on other smart ways to minimize the drudgery of data entry, such as filling out a series of entries with the AutoFill and Flash Fill features as well as entering the same thing in a bunch of cells all at the same time.

After discovering how to fill a worksheet with all this raw data, you find out what has to be the most important lesson of all — how to save all that information on disk so that you don't ever have to enter the stuff again!

So What Ya Gonna Put in That New Workbook of Yours?

When you launch Excel 2013, an Excel 2013 start screen similar to the one shown in Figure 2-1 appears, separated into two panes. In the left pane, Excel lists the names of recently edited workbooks (if any). Below that, the left pane contains an Open Other Workbooks link.

Figure 2-1: The Excel 2013 start screen that appears when you first launch the program.

In the pane on the right side of the start screen, Excel displays thumbnail images of various templates that you can use when starting a new workbook. Templates create new workbooks that follow a particular form such as a budget or inventory list. These new workbooks generated from a template contain ready-made tables and lists often with sample data and headings that you can then edit and change as needed. Then, when you finish, you can save the new customized workbook with a new filename.

The template thumbnails begin with a Blank Workbook template immediately followed by a Take a Tour template. After that, you find thumbnails for a bunch of commonly used workbooks, ranging from budgets to calendars. If none of the example workbooks offered by this list of templates suits your needs, you can use the Search Online Templates text box to find many more templates of a specific type. Right below, you can also click any of the links (Budget, Invoice, Calendars, and so on) in the Suggested Searches to bring up and display a whole hoard of templates of a particular type.

I highly recommend opening the Take a Tour template at some point early in your exploration of Excel 2013. When you click its template thumbnail, Excel immediately opens a new Welcome to Excel1 workbook replete with five worksheets: Start, Fill, Analyze, Chart, and Learn More. The Fill worksheet lets you try out the new Flash Fill feature discussed later in this chapter. The Analyze worksheet lets you experiment with the new Quick Analysis feature covered in Chapter 3. The Chart worksheet lets you test the new Recommended Charts. After playing with any or all of these new features, you can close the Welcome to Excel1 workbook without saving your changes.

When you select one of the template thumbnails in the Excel 2013 start screen other than Blank Workbook and Take a Tour, Excel opens a dialog box that contains a larger version of the template thumbnail along with the name, a brief description, download size, and rating. To then download the template and create a new workbook from it in Excel, click the Create button. If, on perusing the information in this dialog box, you decide that this isn't the template you want to use after all, click the Close button or simply press Esc.

To start a new workbook devoid of any labels and data, click the Blank Workbook template in the Excel 2013 start screen. When you do, Excel opens a new workbook automatically named Book1. This workbook contains a single blank worksheet, automatically named Sheet1. To begin to work on a new spreadsheet, simply start entering information in the Sheet1 worksheet of the Book1 workbook window.

The ins and outs of data entry

Here are a few simple guidelines (a kind of data-entry etiquette, if you will) to keep in mind when you create a spreadsheet in Sheet1 of your new blank workbook:

- ✔ Whenever you can, organize your information in tables of data that use adjacent (neighboring) columns and rows. Start the tables in the upper-left corner of the worksheet and work your way down the sheet, rather than across the sheet, whenever possible. When it's practical, separate each table by no more than a single column or row.

- ✔ When you set up these tables, don't skip columns and rows just to "space out" the information. In Chapter 3, you see how to place as much white space as you want between information in adjacent columns and rows by widening columns, heightening rows, and changing the alignment.

- ✔ Reserve a single column at the left edge of the table for the table's row headings.

- ✔ Reserve a single row at the top of the table for the table's column headings.

- ✔ If your table requires a title, put the title in the row above the column headings. Put the title in the same column as the row headings. You can get information on how to center this title across the columns of the entire table in Chapter 3.

In Chapter 1, I make a big deal about how big each of the worksheets in a workbook is. You may wonder why I'm now on your case about not using that space to spread out the data that you enter into it. After all, given all the real estate that comes with each Excel worksheet, you'd think conserving space would be one of the last things you'd have to worry about.

You'd be 100 percent correct . . . except for one little, itty-bitty thing: Space conservation in the worksheet equals memory conservation. You see, while a table of data grows and expands into columns and rows in new areas of the worksheet, Excel decides that it had better reserve a certain amount of computer memory and hold it open just in case you go crazy and fill that area with cell entries. Therefore, if you skip columns and rows that you really don't need to skip (just to cut down on all that cluttered data), you end up wasting computer memory that could store more information in the worksheet.

You must remember this . . .

Now you know: The amount of computer memory available to Excel determines the ultimate size of the spreadsheet you can build, not the total number of cells in the worksheets of your workbook. When you run out of memory, you've effectively run out of space — no matter how many columns and rows are still available. To maximize the information you can get into a single worksheet, always adopt the "covered wagon" approach to worksheet design by keeping your data close together.

Doing the Data-Entry Thing

Begin by reciting (in unison) the basic rule of worksheet data entry. All together now:

> To enter data in a worksheet, position the cell pointer in the cell where you want the data and then begin typing the entry.

Before you can position the cell pointer in the cell where you want the entry, Excel must be in Ready mode (look for Ready as the Program indicator at the beginning of the Status bar). When you start typing the entry, however, Excel goes through a mode change from Ready to Enter (and *Enter* replaces *Ready* as the Program indicator). If you're not in Ready mode, try pressing Esc on your keyboard.

And if you're doing data entry on a worksheet on a device that doesn't have a physical keyboard, for heaven's sake, open the virtual keyboard and keep it open (preferably floating) in the Excel window during the whole time you're doing data entry. (See "Tips on using the Touch keyboard" in Chapter 1 for details on displaying and using the virtual keyboard on a touchscreen device.)

As soon as you begin typing in Enter mode, the characters that you type in a cell in the worksheet area simultaneously appear on the Formula bar near the top of the screen. Typing something in the current cell also triggers a change to the Formula bar because two new buttons, Cancel and Enter, appear between the Name box drop-down button and the Insert Function button.

As you continue to type, Excel displays your progress on the Formula bar and in the active cell in the worksheet (see Figure 2-2). However, the insertion point (the flashing vertical bar that acts as your cursor) appears only at the end of the characters displayed in the cell.

Enter

Cancel | Insert function

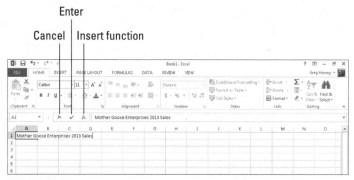

Figure 2-2: What you type appears both in the current cell and on the Formula bar.

After you finish typing your cell entry, you still have to get it into the cell so that it stays put. When you do this, you also change the program from Enter mode back to Ready mode so that you can move the cell pointer to another cell and, perhaps, enter or edit the data there.

To complete your cell entry and, at the same time, get Excel out of Enter mode and back into Ready mode, you can select the Enter button on the Formula bar or press the Enter key or one of the arrow keys (↓, ↑, →, or ←) on your physical or virtual keyboard. You can also press the Tab key or Shift+Tab keys to complete a cell entry.

When you complete a cell entry with any of the keyboard keys — Enter, Tab, Shift+Tab, or any of the arrow keys — you not only complete the entry in the current cell but get the added advantage of moving the cell pointer to a neighboring cell in the worksheet that requires editing or data entry.

Now, even though each of these alternatives gets your text into the cell, each does something a little different afterward, so please take note:

- ✔ If you select the Enter button (the one with the check mark) on the Formula bar, the text goes into the cell, and the cell pointer just stays in the cell containing the brand-new entry.

- ✔ If you press the Enter key on your physical or virtual keyboard, the text goes into the cell, and the cell pointer moves down to the cell below in the next row.

- ✔ If you press one of the arrow keys, the text goes into the cell, and the cell pointer moves to the next cell in the direction of the arrow. Press ↓, and the cell pointer moves below in the next row just as it does when you finish off a cell entry with the Enter key. Press → to move the cell pointer right to the cell in the next column; press ← to move the cell pointer left to the cell in the previous column; and press ↑ to move the cell pointer up to the cell in the next row above.

- ✔ If you press Tab, the text goes into the cell, and the cell pointer moves to the adjacent cell in the column on the immediate right (the same as pressing the → key). If you press Shift+Tab, the cell pointer moves to the adjacent cell in the column on the immediate left (the same as pressing the ← key) after putting in the text.

No matter which of the methods you choose when putting an entry in its place, as soon as you complete your entry in the current cell, Excel deactivates the Formula bar by removing the Cancel and Enter buttons. Thereafter, the data you entered continues to appear in the cell in the worksheet (with certain exceptions that I discuss later in this chapter), and every time you put the cell pointer into that cell, the data will reappear on the Formula bar as well.

If, while still typing an entry or after finishing typing but prior to completing the entry, you realize that you're just about to stick it in the wrong cell, you can clear and deactivate the Formula bar by selecting the Cancel button (the one with the X in it) or by pressing Esc on your keyboard. If, however, you don't realize that you had the wrong cell until after you enter your data there, you have to either move the entry to the correct cell or delete the entry and then re-enter the data in the correct cell.

It Takes All Types

Unbeknownst to you while you go about happily entering data in your spreadsheet, Excel constantly analyzes the stuff you type and classifies it into one of three possible data types: a piece of *text,* a *value,* or a *formula.*

If Excel finds that the entry is a formula, the program automatically calculates the formula and displays the computed result in the worksheet cell (you continue to see the formula itself, however, on the Formula bar). If Excel is satisfied that the entry does not qualify as a formula (I give you the qualifications for an honest-to-goodness formula a little later in this chapter), the program then determines whether the entry should be classified as text or as a value.

Excel makes this distinction between text and values so that it knows how to align the entry in the worksheet. It aligns text entries with the left edge of the cell and values with the right edge. Because most formulas work properly only when they are fed values, by differentiating text from values, the program knows which will and will not work in the formulas that you build. Suffice to say that you can foul up your formulas but good if they refer to any cells containing text where Excel expects values to be.

The telltale signs of text

A text entry is simply an entry that Excel can't pigeonhole as either a formula or value. This makes text the catchall category of Excel data types. As a practical rule, most text entries (also known as *labels*) are a combination of letters and punctuation or letters and numbers. Text is used mostly for titles, headings, and notes in the worksheet.

You can tell right away whether Excel has accepted a cell entry as text because text entries automatically align at the left edge of their cells. If the text entry is wider than the cell can display, the data spills into the neighboring cell or cells on the right, *as long as those cells remain blank.*

If, sometime later, you enter information in a cell that contains spillover text from a cell to its left, Excel cuts off the spillover of the long text entry (see Figure 2-3). Not to worry: Excel doesn't actually lop these characters off the cell entry — it simply shaves the display to make room for the new entry. To redisplay the seemingly missing portion of the long text entry, you have to widen the column that contains the cell where the text is entered. (To find out how to do this, skip ahead to Chapter 3.)

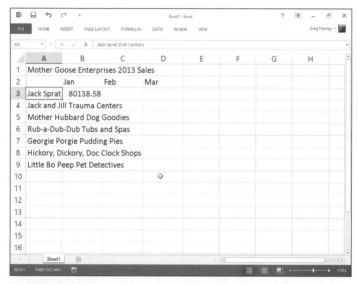

Figure 2-3: Entries in cells to the right cut off the spillover text in cells on the left.

How Excel evaluates its values

Values are the building blocks of most of the formulas that you create in Excel. As such, values come in two flavors: numbers that represent quantities (*14* stores or *$140,000* dollars) and numbers that represent dates (*July 30, 1995*) or times (*2* p.m.).

You can tell whether Excel has accepted your entry as a value because values automatically align at the right edge of their cells. If the value that you enter is wider than the column containing the cell can display, Excel automatically converts the value to (of all things) *scientific notation.* To restore a value that's been converted into that weird scientific notation stuff to a regular number, simply widen the column for that cell. (Read how in Chapter 3.)

Verifying Excel's got your number

When building a new worksheet, you'll probably spend a lot of your time entering numbers, representing all types of quantities from money that you made (or lost) to the percentage of the office budget that went to coffee and donuts. (You mean you don't get donuts?)

To enter a numeric value that represents a positive quantity, like the amount of money you made last year, just select a cell, type the numbers — for example, **459600** — and complete the entry in the cell by clicking the Enter button, pressing the Enter key, and so on. To enter a numeric value that represents a negative quantity, such as the amount of money the office spent on coffee and donuts last year, begin the entry with the minus sign or hyphen (–) before typing the numbers and then complete the entry. For example, **–175** (that's not too much to spend on coffee and donuts when you just made $459,600).

If you're trained in accounting, you can enclose the negative number (that's *expense* to you) in parentheses. You'd enter it like this: **(175)**. If you go to all the trouble to use parentheses for your negatives (expenses), Excel goes ahead and automatically converts the number so that it begins with a minus sign; if you enter **(175)** in the Coffee and Donut expense cell, Excel spits back –175. (Relax, you can find out how to get your beloved parentheses back for the expenses in your spreadsheet in Chapter 3.)

With numeric values that represent dollar amounts, like the amount of money you made last year, you can include dollar signs ($) and commas (,) just as they appear in the printed or handwritten numbers you're working from. Just be aware that when you enter a number with commas, Excel assigns a number format to the value that matches your use of commas. (For more information on number formats and how they are used, see Chapter 3.) Likewise, when you preface a financial figure with a dollar sign, Excel assigns an appropriate dollar-number format to the value (one that automatically inserts commas between the thousands).

When entering numeric values with decimal places, use the period as the decimal point. When you enter decimal values, the program automatically adds a zero before the decimal point (Excel inserts 0.34 in a cell when you enter **.34**) and drops trailing zeros entered after the decimal point (Excel inserts 12.5 in a cell when you enter **12.50**).

If you don't know the decimal equivalent for a value that contains a fraction, you can just go ahead and enter the value with its fraction. For example, if you don't know that 2.1875 is the decimal equivalent for 2³⁄₁₆, just type **2 ³⁄₁₆** (making sure to add a space between the 2 and 3) in the cell. After completing the entry, when you put the cell pointer in that cell, you see 2³⁄₁₆ in the cell of the worksheet, but 2.1875 appears on the Formula bar. As you see in Chapter 3, it's then a simple trick to format the display of 2³⁄₁₆ in the cell so that it matches the 2.1875 on the Formula bar.

If you need to enter simple fractions, such as ¾ or ⅝, you must enter them as a mixed number preceded by zero; for example, enter **0 3⁄4** or **0 5⁄8** (be sure to include a space between the zero and the fraction). Otherwise, Excel thinks that you're entering the dates March 4 (3/4) or May 8 (5/8).

When entering in a cell a numeric value that represents a percentage (so much out of a hundred), you have this choice:

✔ You can divide the number by 100 and enter the decimal equivalent (by moving the decimal point two places to the left like your teacher taught you; for example, enter **.12** for 12 percent).

✔ You can enter the number with the percent sign (for example, enter **12%**).

Either way, Excel stores the decimal value in the cell (0.12 in this example). If you use the percent sign, Excel assigns a percentage-number format to the value in the worksheet so that it appears as 12%.

How to fix your decimal places (when you don't even know they're broken)

If you find that you need to enter a whole slew of numbers that use the same number of decimal places, you can turn on Excel's Fixed Decimal setting and have the program enter the decimals for you. This feature really comes in handy when you have to enter hundreds of financial figures that all use two decimal places (for example, for the number of cents).

To *fix* the number of decimal places in a numeric entry, follow these steps:

1. **Choose File⇨Options⇨Advanced or press Alt+FTA.**

   The Advanced tab of the Excel Options dialog box opens.

2. **Select the Automatically Insert a Decimal Point check box in the Editing Options section to fill it with a check mark.**

   By default, Excel fixes the decimal place two places to the left of the last number you type. To change the default Places setting, go to Step 3; otherwise move to Step 4.

3. **(Optional) Select or enter a new number in the Places text box or use the spinner buttons to change the value.**

   For example, you could change the Places setting to 3 to enter numbers with the following decimal placement: 00.000.

4. **Click OK or press Enter.**

   Excel displays the Fixed Decimal status indicator on the Status bar to let you know that the Fixed Decimal feature is now active.

After fixing the decimal place in numeric values, Excel automatically adds a decimal point to any numeric value that you enter using the number of places you selected; all you do is type the digits and complete the entry in the cell. For example, to enter the numeric value 100.99 in a cell after fixing the decimal point to two places, type the digits **10099** without adding any period for a decimal point. When you complete the cell entry, Excel automatically inserts a decimal point two places from the right in the number you typed, leaving 100.99 in the cell.

When you're ready to return to normal data entry for numerical values (where you enter any decimal points yourself), open the Advanced tab of the Excel Options dialog box (Alt+FTA), select the Automatically Insert a Decimal Point check box again, this time to clear it, and then click OK or press Enter. Excel removes the Fixed Decimal indicator from the Status bar.

Tapping on the old ten-key

You can make the Fixed Decimal feature work even better when entering numeric data on a physical keyboard that has a separate ten-key numeric keypad. All you do is select the block of cells where you want to enter numbers (see "Entries all around the block," later in this chapter) and then press Num Lock so that you can enter all the data for this cell selection from the numeric keypad (à la ten-key adding machine).

Using this approach, all you have to do to enter the range of values in each cell is type the number's digits and press Enter on the numeric keypad. Excel inserts the decimal point in the proper place while it moves the cell pointer down to the next cell. Even better, when you finish entering the last value in a column, pressing Enter automatically moves the cell pointer to the cell at the top of the next column in the selection.

Look at Figures 2-4 and 2-5 to see how you can make the ten-key method work for you. In Figure 2-4, the Fixed Decimal feature is turned on (using the default of two decimal places), and the block of cells from B3 through D9 is selected. You also see that six entries have already been made in cells B3 through B8 and a seventh, 30834.63, is about to be completed in cell B9. To make this entry when the Fixed Decimal feature is on, you simply type **3083463** from the numeric keypad.

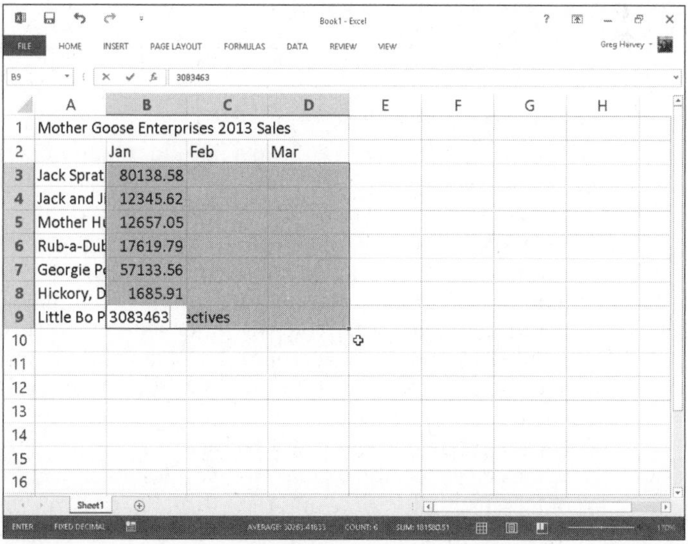

Figure 2-4: To enter the value 30834.63 in cell B9, type **3083463** and press Enter.

In Figure 2-5, check out what happens when you press Enter (on either the regular keyboard or the numeric keypad). Not only does Excel automatically add the decimal point to the value in cell B9, but it also moves the cell pointer up and over to cell C3 where you can continue entering the values for this column.

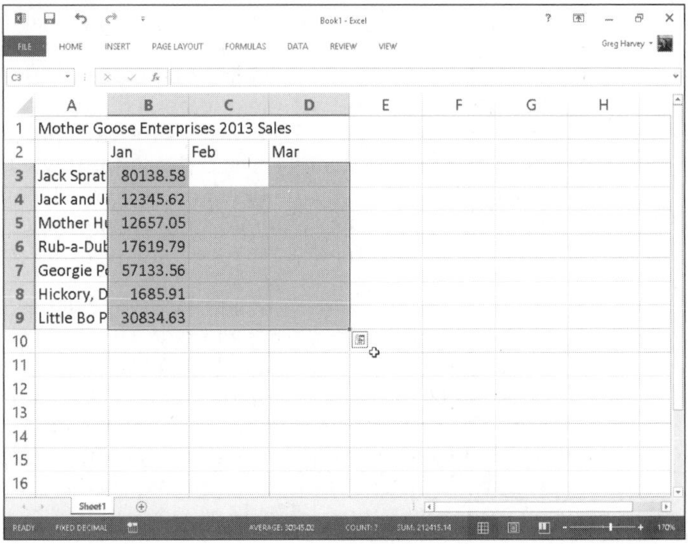

Figure 2-5: Press Enter to complete the 30834.63 entry in cell B9. Excel automatically moves the cell pointer up and over to cell C3.

Entering dates with no debate

At first look, it may strike you a bit odd to enter dates and times as values in the cells of a worksheet rather than text. The reason for this is simple, really: Dates and times entered as values can be used in formula calculations, whereas dates and times entered as text cannot. For example, if you enter two dates as values, you can then set up a formula that subtracts the more recent date from the older date and returns the number of days between them. This kind of thing just couldn't happen if you were to enter the two dates as text entries.

Excel determines whether the date or time that you type is a value or text by the format that you follow. If you follow one of Excel's built-in date-and-time formats, the program recognizes the date or time as a value. If you don't follow one of the

built-in formats, the program enters the date or time as a text
entry — it's as simple as that.

Excel recognizes the following time formats:

3 AM or **3 PM**

3 A or **3 P** (upper- or lowercase a or p — Excel inserts
3:00 AM or 3:00 PM)

3:21 AM or **3:21 PM** (upper- or lowercase am or pm)

3:21:04 AM or **3:21:04 PM** (upper- or lowercase am or pm)

15:21

15:21:04

Excel isn't fussy, so you can enter the AM or PM designation
in the date in any manner — uppercase letters, lowercase
letters, or even a mix of the two.

Excel knows the following date formats. (Month abbreviations
always use the first three letters of the name of the month:
Jan, Feb, Mar, and so forth.)

November 6, 2012 or **November 6, 12** (appear in cell as
6-Nov-12

11/6/12 or **11-6-12** (appear in cell as 11/6/2012)

6-Nov-12 or **6/Nov/12** or even **6Nov12** (all appear in cell
as 6-Nov-12)

11/6 or **6-Nov** or **6/Nov** or **6Nov** (all appear in cell as 6-Nov)

Nov-06 or **Nov/06** or **Nov06** (all appear in cell as 6-Nov)

Make it a date in the 21st Century

Contrary to what you might think, when entering dates in the
21st Century, you need to enter only the last two digits of
the year. For example, to enter the date January 6, 2012, in a
worksheet, I enter **1/6/12** in the target cell. Likewise, to put
the date February 15, 2013, in a worksheet, I enter **2/15/13** in
the target cell.

Entering only the last two digits of dates in the 21st Century
works only for dates in the first three decades of the new century (2000 through 2029). To enter dates for the years 2030
on, you need to input all four digits of the year.

This also means, however, that to put in dates in the first three decades of the 20th Century (1900 through 1929), you must enter all four digits of the year. For example, to put in the date July 21, 1925, you have to enter **7/21/1925** in the target cell. Otherwise, if you enter just the last two digits (**25**) for the year part of the date, Excel enters a date for the year 2025 and not 1925!

Excel 2013 always displays all four digits of the year in the cell and on the Formula bar even when you only enter the last two. For example, if you enter **11/06/12** in a cell, Excel automatically displays 11/6/2012 in the worksheet cell (and on the Formula bar when that cell is current).

Therefore, by looking at the Formula bar, you can always tell when you've entered a 20th rather than a 21st Century date in a cell even if you can't keep straight the rules for when to enter just the last two digits rather than all four. (Read Chapter 3 for information on how to format your date entries so that only the last digits display in the worksheet.)

For information on how to perform simple arithmetic operations between the dates and time you enter in a worksheet and have the results make sense, see the information about dates in Chapter 3.

Fabricating those fabulous formulas!

As entries go in Excel, formulas are the real workhorses of the worksheet. If you set up a formula properly, it computes the correct answer when you enter the formula into a cell. From then on, the formula stays up to date, recalculating the results whenever you change any of the values that the formula uses.

You let Excel know that you're about to enter a formula (rather than some text or a value), in the current cell by starting the formula with the equal sign (=). Most simple formulas follow the equal sign with a built-in function, such as SUM or AVERAGE. (See the section "Inserting a function into a formula with the Insert Function button," later in this chapter, for more information on using functions in formulas.) Other simple formulas use a series of values or cell references that contain values separated by one or more of the following mathematical operators:

+ (plus sign) for addition

– (minus sign or hyphen) for subtraction

* (asterisk) for multiplication

/ (slash) for division

^ (caret) for raising a number to an exponential power

For example, to create a formula in cell C2 that multiplies a value entered in cell A2 by a value in cell B2, enter the following formula in cell C2: =**A2*B2**.

To enter this formula in cell C2, follow these steps:

1. **Select cell C2.**

2. **Type the entire formula** =A2*B2 **in the cell.**

3. **Press Enter.**

Or

1. **Select cell C2.**

2. **Type** = **(equal sign).**

3. **Select cell A2 in the worksheet by using the mouse or the keyboard.**

   This action places the cell reference A2 in the formula in the cell (as shown in Figure 2-6).

4. **Type * (Shift+8 on the top row of the keyboard).**

   The asterisk is used for multiplication rather than the × symbol you used in school.

5. **Select cell B2 in the worksheet with the mouse, keyboard, or by tapping it on the screen (when using a touchscreen device).**

   This action places the cell reference B2 in the formula (as shown in Figure 2-7).

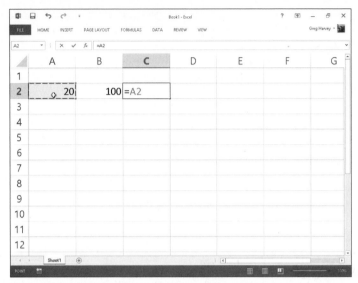

Figure 2-6: To start the formula, type = and then select cell A2.

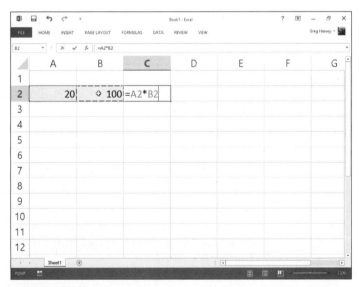

Figure 2-7: To complete the second part of the formula, type * and select cell B2.

6. Click the Enter button on the Formula bar to complete the formula entry while keeping the cell pointer in cell C2.

Excel displays the calculated answer in cell C2 and the formula =A2*B2 in the Formula bar (as shown in Figure 2-8).

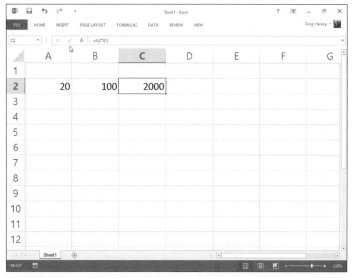

Figure 2-8: Click the Enter button, and Excel displays the answer in cell C2 while the formula appears in the Formula bar above.

When you finish entering the formula **=A2*B2** in cell C2 of the worksheet, Excel displays the calculated result, depending on the values currently entered in cells A2 and B2. The major strength of the electronic spreadsheet is the capability of formulas to change their calculated results automatically to match changes in the cells referenced by the formulas.

Now comes the fun part: After creating a formula like the preceding one that refers to the values in certain cells (rather than containing those values itself), you can change the values in those cells, and Excel automatically recalculates the formula, using these new values and displaying the updated answer in the worksheet! Using the example shown in Figure 2-8, suppose that you change the value in cell B2 from 100 to 50. The moment that you complete this change in cell B2, Excel recalculates the formula and displays the new answer, 1000, in cell C2.

If you want it, just point it out

The method of selecting the cells you use in a formula, rather than typing their cell references, is *pointing*. On most devices on which you're running Excel 2013, pointing is quicker than typing and certainly reduces the risk that you might mistype a cell reference. When you type a cell reference, you can easily type the wrong column letter or row number and not realize your mistake by looking at the calculated result returned in the cell. But when you directly select the cell that you want to use in a formula (by clicking or tapping it or even using the arrow keys to move the cell cursor to it), you have less chance of entering the wrong cell reference.

On a small handheld device with a tiny touchscreen such as a smartphone, sliding to scroll to the proper column and row and then tapping the cell to select and add its reference to a new formula may be even more challenging than typing the formula's cell references on the device's virtual keyboard. This is when I recommend typing instead of pointing for creating new formulas. Just be aware that when you type the first letter of your cell's column reference into a formula, Excel automatically displays a list of all the built-in functions whose names start with that letter. This list immediately disappears as soon as you type the second letter of the column (if the cell has one) or the first digit of its row number. Also, be sure to double-check that the cell references you type into the formula refer to the cells you really want to use.

Altering the natural order of operations

Many formulas that you create perform more than one mathematical operation. Excel performs each operation, moving from left to right, according to a strict pecking order (the natural order of arithmetic operations). In this order, multiplication and division pull more weight than addition and subtraction and, therefore, perform first, even if these operations don't come first in the formula (when reading from left to right).

Consider the series of operations in the following formula:

```
=A2+B2*C2
```

If cell A2 contains the number 5, B2 contains the number 10, and C2 contains the number 2, Excel evaluates the following formula:

```
=5+10*2
```

In this formula, Excel multiplies 10 times 2 to equal 20 and then adds this result to 5 to produce the result 25.

If you want Excel to perform the addition between the values in cells A2 and B2 before the program multiplies the result by the value in cell C2, enclose the addition operation in parentheses as follows:

```
=(A2+B2)*C2
```

The parentheses around the addition tell Excel that you want this operation performed before the multiplication. If cell A2 contains the number 5, B2 contains the number 10, and C2 contains the number 2, Excel adds 5 and 10 to equal 15 and then multiplies this result by 2 to produce the result 30.

In fancier formulas, you may need to add more than one set of parentheses, one within another (like the wooden Russian dolls that nest within each other) to indicate the order in which you want the calculations to take place. When nesting parentheses, Excel first performs the calculation contained in the most inside pair of parentheses and then uses that result in further calculations as the program works its way outward. For example, consider the following formula:

```
=(A4+(B4-C4))*D4
```

Excel first subtracts the value in cell C4 from the value in cell B4, adds the difference to the value in cell A4, and then finally multiplies that sum by the value in D4.

Without the additions of the two sets of nested parentheses, left to its own devices, Excel would first multiply the value in cell C4 by that in D4, add the value in A4 to that in B4, and then perform the subtraction.

Don't worry too much when nesting parentheses in a formula if you don't pair them properly so that you have a right parenthesis for every left parenthesis in the formula. If you do not include a right parenthesis for every left one, Excel displays an alert dialog box that suggests the correction needed to balance the pairs. If you agree with the program's suggested correction, you simply click the Yes button. However, be sure that you only use parentheses: ( ). Excel balks at the use of brackets — [ ] — or braces — { } — in a formula by giving you an Error alert box.

Formula flub-ups

Under certain circumstances, even the best formulas can appear to have freaked out after you get them in your worksheet. You can tell right away that a formula's gone haywire because instead of the nice calculated value you expected to see in the cell, you get a strange, incomprehensible message in all uppercase letters beginning with the number sign (#) and ending with an exclamation point (!) or, in one case, a question mark (?). This weirdness, in the parlance of spreadsheets, is as an *error value.* Its purpose is to let you know that some element — either in the formula itself or in a cell referred to by the formula — is preventing Excel from returning the anticipated calculated value.

 When one of your formulas returns one of these error values, an alert indicator (in the form of an exclamation point in a diamond) appears to the left of the cell when it contains the cell pointer, and the upper-left corner of the cell contains a tiny green triangle. When you position the mouse pointer on this alert indicator, Excel displays a brief description of the formula error and adds a drop-down button to the immediate right of its box. When you click this button, a pop-up menu appears with a number of related options. To access online help on this formula error, including suggestions on how to get rid of the error, click the Help on This Error item on this pop-up menu.

The worst thing about error values is that they can contaminate other formulas in the worksheet. If a formula returns an error value to a cell and a second formula in another cell refers to the value calculated by the first formula, the second formula returns the same error value, and so on down the line.

After an error value shows up in a cell, you have to discover what caused the error and edit the formula in the worksheet. In Table 2-1, I list some error values that you might run into in a worksheet and then explain the most common causes.

Table 2-1	Error Values That You May Encounter from Faulty Formulas
What Shows Up in the Cell	*What's Going On Here?*
#DIV/0!	Appears when the formula calls for division by a cell that either contains the value 0 or, as is more often the case, is empty. Division by zero is a no-no in mathematics.
#NAME?	Appears when the formula refers to a *range name* that doesn't exist in the worksheet. This error value appears when you type the wrong range name or fail to enclose in quotation marks some text used in the formula, causing Excel to think that the text refers to a range name.
#NULL!	Appears most often when you insert a space (where you should have used a comma) to separate cell references used as arguments for functions.
#NUM!	Appears when Excel encounters a problem with a number in the formula, such as the wrong type of argument in an Excel function or a calculation that produces a number too large or too small to be represented in the worksheet.
#REF!	Appears when Excel encounters an invalid cell reference, such as when you delete a cell referred to in a formula or paste cells over the cells referred to in a formula.
#VALUE!	Appears when you use the wrong type of argument or operator in a function, or when you call for a mathematical operation that refers to cells that contain text entries.

Fixing Those Data Entry Flub-Ups

We all wish we were perfect, but alas, because so few of us are, we are best off preparing for those inevitable times when we mess up. When entering vast quantities of data, it's easy for those nasty little typos to creep into your work. In your pursuit of the perfect spreadsheet, here are things you can do. First, get Excel to correct certain data entry typos automatically when they happen with its AutoCorrect feature. Second, manually correct any disgusting little errors that get through, either while you're still in the process of making the entry in the cell or after the entry has gone in.

You really AutoCorrect that for me

The AutoCorrect feature is a godsend for those of us who tend to make the same stupid typos over and over. With AutoCorrect, you can alert Excel 2013 to your own particular typing gaffes and tell the program how it should automatically fix them for you.

When you first install Excel, the AutoCorrect feature already knows to automatically correct two initial capital letters in an entry (by lowercasing the second capital letter), to capitalize the name of the days of the week, and to replace a set number of text entries and typos with particular substitute text.

You can add to the list of text replacements at any time when using Excel. These text replacements can be of two types: typos that you routinely make along with the correct spelling, and abbreviations or acronyms that you type all the time along with their full forms.

To add to the replacements, follow these steps:

1. **Choose File⇨Options⇨Proofing or press Alt+FTP and then click the AutoCorrect Options button or press Alt+A.**

   Excel opens the AutoCorrect dialog box shown in Figure 2-9.

2. **On the AutoCorrect tab in this dialog box, enter the typo or abbreviation in the Replace text box.**

3. **Enter the correction or full form in the With text box.**

4. **Click the Add button or press Enter to add the new typo or abbreviation to the AutoCorrect list.**

5. **Click the OK button to close the AutoCorrect dialog box.**

Figure 2-9: Use the Replace and With options in the AutoCorrect dialog box to add all typos and abbreviations you want Excel to automatically correct or fill out.

Cell editing etiquette

Despite the help of AutoCorrect, some mistakes are bound to get you. How you correct them really depends upon whether you notice before or after completing the cell entry.

- ✔ If you catch the mistake before you complete an entry, you can delete it by pressing your Backspace key until you remove all the incorrect characters from the cell. Then you can retype the rest of the entry or the formula before you complete the entry in the cell.

- ✔ If you don't discover the mistake until after you've completed the cell entry, you have a choice of replacing the whole thing or editing just the mistakes.

- ✔ When dealing with short entries, you'll probably want to take the replacement route. To replace a cell entry, position the cell pointer in that cell, type your replacement entry, and then click the Enter button or press Enter.

- ✔ When the error in an entry is relatively easy to fix and the entry is on the long side, you'll probably want to edit the cell entry rather than replace it. To edit the entry in the cell, simply double-click or double-tap the cell or select the cell and then press F2.

- ✔ Doing either one reactivates the Formula bar by displaying the Enter and Cancel buttons once again and placing the insertion point in the cell entry in the worksheet. (If you double-click or double-tap, the insertion point positions itself wherever you click; press F2, and the insertion point positions itself after the last character in the entry.)

✔ Notice also that the mode indicator changes to Edit. While in this mode, you can use the mouse or the arrow keys to position the insertion point at the place in the cell entry that needs fixing.

In Table 2-2, I list the keystrokes that you can use to reposition the insertion point in the cell entry and delete unwanted characters. If you want to insert new characters at the insertion point, simply start typing. If you want to delete existing characters at the insertion point while you type new ones, press the Insert key on your keyboard to switch from the normal insert mode to overtype mode. To return to normal insert mode, press Insert a second time. When you finish making corrections to the cell entry, you must complete the edits by pressing Enter before Excel updates the contents of the cell.

While Excel is in Edit mode, you must re-enter the edited cell contents by either clicking the Enter button or pressing Enter. You can use the arrow keys as a way to complete an entry only when the program is in Enter mode. When the program is in Edit mode, the arrow keys move the insertion point only through the entry that you're editing, not to a new cell.

Table 2-2	Keystrokes for Fixing Those Cell Entry Flub-Ups
Keystroke	*What the Keystroke Does*
Delete	Deletes the character to the right of the insertion point
Backspace	Deletes the character to the left of the insertion point
→	Positions the insertion point one character to the right
←	Positions the insertion point one character to the left
↑	Positions the insertion point, when it is at the end of the cell entry, to its preceding position to the left
End or ↓	Moves the insertion point after the last character in the cell entry

Keystroke	What the Keystroke Does
Home	Moves the insertion point in front of the first character of the cell entry
Ctrl+→	Positions the insertion point in front of the next word in the cell entry
Ctrl+←	Positions the insertion point in front of the preceding word in the cell entry
Insert	Switches between insert and overtype mode

Taking the Drudgery out of Data Entry

Before leaving the topic of data entry, I feel duty-bound to cover some of the shortcuts that really help to cut down on the drudgery of this task. These data-entry tips include the AutoComplete, AutoFill, and Flash Fill features as well as doing data entry in a preselected block of cells and making the same entry in a bunch of cells all at the same time.

I'm just not complete without you

AutoComplete is like a moronic mind reader who anticipates what you might want to enter next based on what you just entered. This feature comes into play only when you're entering a column of text entries. (It does not come into play when entering values or formulas or when entering a row of text entries.) When entering a column of text entries, AutoComplete looks at the kinds of entries that you make in that column and automatically duplicates them in subsequent rows whenever you start a new entry that begins with the same letter as an existing entry.

For example, suppose that I enter **Capital Investments** (one of the many investment firms that our company uses) in cell A2 and then move the cell pointer down to cell A3 in the row below and press **C** (lowercase or uppercase, it doesn't matter). AutoComplete immediately inserts the remainder of the familiar entry — *apital Investments* — in this cell after the C.

Now this is great if I happen to need Capital Investments as the row heading in both cells A2 and A3. Anticipating that I might be typing a different entry that just happens to start with the same letter as the one above, AutoComplete automatically selects everything after the first letter in the duplicated entry it inserted (from *apital* on, in this example). This enables me to replace the duplicate text supplied by AutoComplete just by continuing to type.

If you override a duplicate supplied by AutoComplete in a column by typing one of your own (as in the example of the Capital Investments entry automatically corrected to Cook Investments in cell A3), you effectively shut down its capability to supply any more duplicates for that particular letter. For instance, in my example, after changing Capital Investments to Cook Investments in cell A3, AutoComplete doesn't do anything if I then type **C** in cell A4. In other words, you're on your own if you don't continue to accept AutoComplete's typing suggestions.

If you find that the AutoComplete feature is really making it hard for you to enter a series of cell entries that all start with the same letter but are otherwise not alike, you can turn off the AutoComplete feature. Select File⇨Options⇨Advanced or press Alt+FTA to open the Advanced tab of the Excel Options dialog box. Then, select the Enable AutoComplete for Cell Values check box in the Editing Options section to remove its check mark before clicking OK.

Fill 'er up with AutoFill

Many of the worksheets that you create with Excel require the entry of a series of sequential dates or numbers. For example, a worksheet may require you to title the columns with the 12 months, from January through December, or to number the rows from 1 to 100.

Excel's AutoFill feature makes short work of this kind of repetitive task. All you have to enter is the starting value for the series. In most cases, AutoFill is smart enough to figure out how to fill out the series for you when you drag the fill handle to the right (to take the series across columns to the right) or down (to extend the series to the rows below).

The AutoFill (or fill) handle looks like this — + — and appears only when you position the mouse (or Touch Pointer on a touchscreen) on the lower-right corner of the active cell (or the last cell, when you've selected a block of cells). If you drag a cell selection with the white-cross mouse pointer rather than the AutoFill handle, Excel simply extends the cell selection to those cells you drag through (see Chapter 3). If you drag a cell selection with the arrowhead pointer, Excel moves the cell selection.

When creating a series with the fill handle, you can drag in only one direction at a time. For example, you can fill the series or copy the entry to the range to the left or right of the cell that contains the initial values, or you can fill the series or copy to the range above or below the cell containing the initial values. You can't, however, fill or copy the series to two directions at the same time (such as down and to the right by dragging the fill handle diagonally).

As you drag the fill handle, the program keeps you informed of whatever entry will be entered into the last cell selected in the range by displaying that entry next to the mouse pointer (a kind of AutoFill tips, if you will). After extending the range with the fill handle, Excel either creates a series in all of the cells that you select or copies the entire range with the initial value. To the right of the last entry in the filled or copied series, Excel also displays a drop-down button that contains a shortcut menu of options. You can use this shortcut menu to override Excel's default filling or copying. For example, when you use the fill handle, Excel copies an initial value into a range of cells. But, if you want a sequential series, you could do this by selecting the Fill Series command on the AutoFill Options shortcut menu.

In Figures 2-10 and 2-11, I illustrate how to use AutoFill to enter a row of months, starting with January in cell B2 and ending with June in cell G2. To do this, simply enter **Jan** in cell B2 and then position the mouse pointer or Touch Pointer on the fill handle in the lower-right corner of this cell before you drag through to cell G2 on the right (as shown in Figure 2-10). When you release the mouse button or remove your finger or stylus from the touchscreen, Excel fills in the names of the rest of the months (Feb through Jun) in the selected cells (as shown in Figure 2-11). Excel keeps the cells with the series of months selected, giving you another chance to modify the series. (If you went too far, you can drag the fill handle to the left to cut back on the list of months; if you didn't go far enough, you can drag it to the right to extend the list of months farther.)

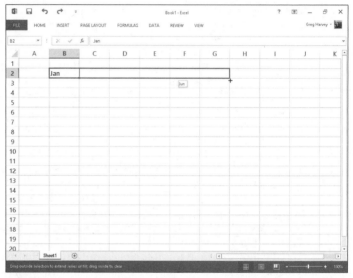

Figure 2-10: To enter a series of months, enter the first month and then drag the fill handle in a direction to add sequential months.

Also, you can use the options on the AutoFill Options drop-down menu shown in Figure 2-11. To display this menu, click the drop-down button that appears on the fill handle (to the right of Jun) to override the series created by default. To have Excel copy Jan into each of the selected cells, choose Copy Cells on this menu. To have the program fill the selected cells with the formatting used in cell B2 (in this case, the cell has had bold applied to it — see Chapter 3 for details on formatting cells), select Fill Formatting Only on this menu. To have Excel fill in the series of months in the selected cells without copying the formatting used in cell B2, select the Fill Without Formatting command from this shortcut menu.

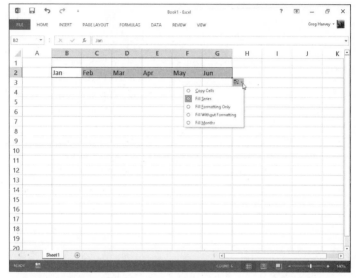

Figure 2-11: Release the mouse button, and Excel fills the cell selection with the missing months.

See Table 2-3 in the following section to see some of the different initial values that AutoFill can use and the types of series that Excel can create from them.

Working with a spaced series

AutoFill uses the initial value that you select (date, time, day, year, and so on) to design the series. All the sample series I show in Table 2-3 change by a factor of one (one day, one month, or one number). You can tell AutoFill to create a series that changes by some other value: Enter two sample values in neighboring cells that describe the amount of change you want between each value in the series. Make these two values the initial selection that you extend with the fill handle.

For example, to start a series with Saturday and enter every other day across a row, enter **Saturday** in the first cell and **Monday** in the cell next door. After selecting both cells, drag the fill handle across the cells to the right as far as you need to fill out a series based on these two initial values. When you release the mouse button or remove your finger or stylus from the screen, Excel follows the example set in the first two cells by entering every other day (Wednesday to the right of Monday, Friday to the right of Wednesday, and so on).

Table 2-3	Samples of Series You Can Create with AutoFill
Value Entered in First Cell	*Extended Series Created by AutoFill in the Next Three Cells*
June	July, August, September
Jun	Jul, Aug, Sep
Tuesday	Wednesday, Thursday, Friday
Tue	Wed, Thu, Fri
4/1/99	4/2/99, 4/3/99, 4/4/99
Jan-00	Feb-00, Mar-00, Apr-00
15-Feb	16-Feb, 17-Feb, 18-Feb
10:00 PM	11:00 PM, 12:00 AM, 1:00 AM
8:01	9:01, 10:01, 11:01
Quarter 1	Quarter 2, Quarter 3, Quarter 4
Qtr2	Qtr3, Qtr4, Qtr1
Q3	Q4, Q1, Q2
Product 1	Product 2, Product 3, Product 4

Copying with AutoFill

You can use AutoFill to copy a text entry throughout a cell range (rather than fill in a series of related entries). To copy a text entry to a cell range, engage the Ctrl key while you click and drag the fill handle. When you do, a plus sign appears to the right of the fill handle — your sign that AutoFill will *copy* the entry in the active cell instead of creating a series using it. You can also tell because the entry that appears as the AutoFill tip next to the mouse or Touch Pointer while you drag contains the same text as the original cell. If you decide after copying an initial label or value to a range that you should have used it to fill in a series, click the drop-down button that appears on the fill handle at the cell with the last copied entry and then select the Fill Series command on the AutoFill Options shortcut menu that appears.

Although holding down Ctrl while you drag the fill handle copies a text entry, just the opposite is true when it comes to values! Suppose that you enter the number **17** in a cell and then drag the fill handle across the row — Excel just copies the number 17 in all the cells that you select. If, however, you hold down Ctrl while you drag the fill handle, Excel then fills out the series (17, 18, 19, and so on). If you forget and create a series of numbers when you only need the value copied, rectify this situation by selecting the Copy Cells command on the AutoFill Options shortcut menu.

Creating custom lists for AutoFill

In addition to varying the increment in a series created with AutoFill, you can also create your own custom series. For example, say your company has offices in the following locations and you get tired of typing the sequence in each new spreadsheet that requires them:

- ✔ New York
- ✔ Chicago
- ✔ Atlanta
- ✔ Seattle
- ✔ San Francisco
- ✔ San Diego

After creating a custom list with these locations, you can enter the entire sequence of cities simply by entering New York in the first cell and then dragging the Fill handle to the blank cells where the rest of the cities should appear.

To create this kind of custom series, follow these steps:

1. **Choose File⇨Options⇨Advanced or press Alt+FTA and then scroll down and click the Edit Custom Lists button in the General section to open the Options dialog box (as shown in Figure 2-12).**

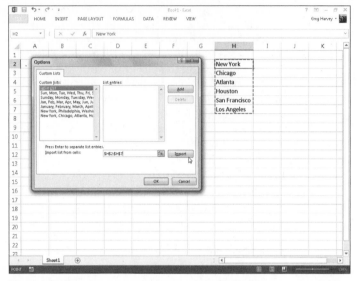

Figure 2-12: Creating a custom company location list from a range of existing cell entries.

If you've already gone to the time and trouble of typing the custom list in a range of cells, go to Step 2. If you haven't yet typed the series in an open worksheet, go to Step 4.

2. **Click in the Import List from Cells text box and then select the range of cells in the worksheet containing the custom list (see Chapter 3 for details).**

   As soon as you start selecting the cells in the worksheet by dragging your mouse or Touch Pointer, Excel automatically collapses the Options dialog box to the minimum to get out of the way. The moment you release the mouse button or remove your finger or stylus from the screen, Excel automatically restores the Options dialog box to its normal size.

3. **Click the Import button to copy this list into the List Entries list box.**

   Skip to Step 6.

4. **Select the List Entries list box and then type each entry (in the desired order), being sure to press Enter after typing each one.**

When all the entries in the custom list appear in the List Entries list box in the order you want them, proceed to Step 5.

5. **Click the Add button to add the list of entries to the Custom Lists list box.**

   Finish creating all the custom lists you need, using the preceding steps. When you're done, move to Step 6.

6. **Click OK twice, the first time to close the Options dialog box and the second to close the Excel Options dialog box and return to the current worksheet in the active workbook.**

After adding a custom list to Excel, from then on you need only enter the first entry in a cell and then use the fill handle to extend it to the cells below or to the right.

If you don't even want to bother with typing the first entry, use the AutoCorrect feature — refer to the section "You really AutoCorrect that for me," earlier in this chapter — to create an entry that fills in as soon as you type your favorite acronym for it (such as *ny* for New York).

Doing AutoFill on a touchscreen

To fill out a data series using your finger or stylus when using Excel on a touchscreen tablet without access to a mouse or touchpad, use the AutoFill button that appears on the mini-toolbar as follows:

1. **Tap the cell containing the initial value in the series you want AutoFill to extend.**

   Excel selects the cell and displays selection handles (with circles) in the upper-left and lower-right corners.

2. **Tap and hold the cell until the mini-toolbar appears.**

   When summoned by touch, the mini-toolbar appears as a single row of command buttons, from Paste to AutoFill, terminated by a Show Context Menu button (with a black triangle pointing downward).

3. **Tap the AutoFill button on the mini-toolbar.**

   Excel closes the mini-toolbar and adds an AutoFill button to the currently selected cell (the blue downward-pointing arrow in square that appears in the lower-right corner of the cell).

4. **Drag the AutoFill button through the blank cells in the same column or row into which the data series sequence is to be filled.**

   As you drag your finger or stylus through blank cells, the Name box on the Formula bar keeps informed of the next entry in the data series. When you release your finger or stylus from the touchscreen after selecting the last blank cell to be filled, Excel fills out the data series in the selected range.

Doing AutoFill with the Fill button on the Home tab

If you're using Excel 2013 on a touchscreen tablet without the benefit of a mouse or touchpad, you can do AutoFill from the Ribbon (you may also want to use this method if you find that using the fill handle to create a series of data entries with AutoFill is too taxing even with a physical mouse).

You simply use the Fill button on the Home tab of the Ribbon to accomplish your AutoFill operations as follows:

1. **Enter the first entry (or entries) upon which the series is to be based in the first cell(s) to hold the new data series in your worksheet.**

2. **Select the cell range where the series is to be created, across a row or down a column, being sure to include the cell with the initial entry or entries in this range.**

3. **Click the Fill button on the Home tab followed by Series on its drop-down menu or press Alt+HFIS.**

   The Fill button is located in the Editing group right below the AutoSum button (the one with the Greek sigma). When you select the Series option, Excel opens the Series dialog box.

4. **Click the AutoFill option button in the Type column followed by the OK button in the Series dialog box.**

   Excel enters a series of data based on the initial value(s) in your selected cell range just as though you'd selected the range with the fill handle.

Note that the Series dialog box contains a bunch of options that you can use to further refine and control the data series that Excel creates. In a linear data series, if you want the series to increment more than one step value at a time, you can increase it in the Step Value text box. Likewise, if you want your linear or AutoFill series to stop when it reaches a particular value, you enter that into the Stop Value text box.

When you're entering a series of dates with AutoFill that increment on anything other than the day, remember the Date Unit options in the Series dialog box enable you to specify other parts of the initial date to increment in the series. Your choices include Weekday, Month, or Year.

Fill it in a flash

Excel's brand new Flash Fill feature gives you the ability to take a part of the data entered into one column of a worksheet table and enter just that data in a new table column using only a few keystrokes. The series of entries appears in the new column, literally in a flash (thus the name, Flash Fill), the moment Excel detects a pattern in your initial data entry that enables it to figure out the data you want to copy. The beauty is that all this happens without the need for you to construct or copy any kind of formula.

The best way to understand Flash Fill is to see it in action. In Figure 2-13, you see a new data table consisting of four columns. The cells in the first column of this table contain the full names of clients (first, middle, and last), all together in one entry. The second, third, and fourth columns need to have just the first, middle, and surnames, respectively, entered into them (so that particular parts of the clients' names can be used in the greetings of form e-mails and letters as in, "Hello Keith," or "Dear Mr. Harper,").

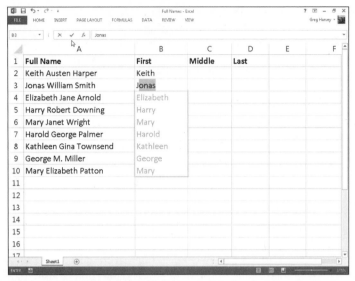

Figure 2-13: Data Table containing full names that need to be split up in separate columns using Flash Fill.

Rather than manually enter the first, middle, or last names in the respective columns (or attempt to copy the entire client name from column A and then edit out the parts not needed in First Name, Middle Name, and Last Name columns), you can use Flash Fill to quickly and effectively do the job. And here's how you do it:

1. **Type** Keith **in cell B2 and complete the entry with the ↓ or Enter key.**

   When you complete this entry with the down-arrow key or Enter key on your keyboard, Excel moves the cell pointer to cell B3 where you only have to type the first letter of the next name for Flash Fill to get the picture.

2. **In Cell B3, only type J, the first letter of the second client's first name.**

   Flash Fill immediately does an AutoFill-type maneuver by suggesting the rest of the second client's first name, Jonas, as the text to enter in this cell. At the same time, Flash Fill suggests entering all the remaining first names from the full names in column A in column B (refer to Figure 2-13).

3. Complete the entry of Jonas in cell B3 by pressing the Enter key or an arrow key.

The moment you complete the data entry in cell B3, the First Name column's done: Excel enters all the other first names in column B at the same time!

To complete this example name table by entering the middle and last names in columns C and D, respectively, you simply repeat these steps in those columns. You enter the first middle name, **Austen**, from cell A2 in cell C2 and then type **W** in cell C3. Complete the entry in cell C3 and the middle name entries in that column are done. Likewise, you enter the first last name, **Harper**, from cell A2 in cell D2 and then type **S** in cell D3. Complete the entry in cell D3, and the last name entries for column D are done, completing the entire data table.

By my count, completing the data entry in this Client Name table required me to make a total of 26 keystrokes, 20 of which were for typing in the first, middle, and last name of the first client along with the initial letters of the first, middle, and last name of the second client and the other six to complete these entries. If Column A of this Client Name table contains the full names of hundreds or even thousands of clients, these 26 keystrokes is insignificant compared to the number that would be required to manually enter their first, middle, and last names in its separate First Name, Middle Name, and Last Name columns or even to edit down copies of the full names in each of them.

Keep in mind that Flash Fill works perfectly at extracting parts of longer data entries in a column provided that all the entries follow the same pattern and use same type of separators (spaces, commas, dashes, and the like). For example, in Figure 2-13, there's an anomaly in the full name entries in cell A9 where only the middle initial with a period is entered instead of the full middle name. In this case, Flash Fill simply enters M in cell C9 and you have to manually edit its entry to add the necessary period. Also, remember that Flash Fill's usefulness isn't restricted to all-text entries as in my example Client Name table. It can also parse entries that mix text and numbers such as part numbers (AJ-1234, RW-8007, and so forth).

Inserting special symbols

Excel makes it easy to enter special symbols, such as foreign currency indicators, and special characters, such as the trademark and copyright symbols, into your cell entries. To add a special symbol or character to a cell entry you're making or editing, select Insert⇨Symbol on the Ribbon or press Alt+NU to open the Symbol dialog box.

The Symbol dialog box contains two tabs: Symbols and Special Characters. To insert a mathematical or foreign currency symbol on the Symbols tab, select its symbol in the list box and then click the Insert button. (You can also do this by double-clicking or double-tapping the symbol.) To insert characters, such as foreign language or accented characters from other character sets, click the Subset drop-down button followed by the name of the set in the drop-down list and the desired characters in the list box. You can also insert commonly used currency and mathematical symbols, such as the pound or plus-or-minus symbol, by selecting them in the Recently Used Symbols section at the bottom of this tab.

To insert special characters, such as the registered trademark, paragraph symbol, and so forth, click the Special Characters tab of the Symbol dialog box followed by the symbol in the scrolling list and the Insert button. (You can insert one of these special characters by double-clicking or double-tapping it also.)

When you finish inserting special symbols and characters, close the Symbol dialog box by pressing Esc or clicking the Close button in its upper-right corner.

Entries all around the block

When you want to enter a table of information in a new worksheet, you can simplify the job of entering the data if you select all the empty cells in which you want to make entries before you begin entering any information. Just position the cell pointer in the first cell of what is to become the data table and then select all the cells in the subsequent columns and rows. (For information on the ways to select a range of cells, see Chapter 3.) After you select the block of cells, you can begin entering the first entry.

When you select a block of cells (also known as a *range*) before you enter information, Excel restricts data entry to that range as follows:

✔ The program automatically advances the cell pointer to the next cell in the range when you click the Enter button on the Formula bar or press the Enter key to complete each cell entry.

✔ In a cell range that contains several different rows and columns, Excel advances the cell pointer down each row of the column while you make your entries. When the cell pointer reaches the cell in the last row of the column, the cell pointer advances to the first selected row in the next column to the right. If the cell range uses only one row, Excel advances the cell pointer from left to right across the row.

✔ When you finish entering information in the last cell in the selected range, Excel positions the cell pointer in the first cell of the now-completed data table. To deselect the cell range, select a single cell in the worksheet (inside or outside the selected range — it doesn't matter) or press one of the arrow keys.

Be sure that you don't press one of the arrow keys to complete a cell entry within a preselected cell range instead of clicking the Enter button or pressing Enter. Pressing an arrow key deselects the range of cells when Excel moves the cell pointer. To move the cell pointer around a cell range without deselecting the range, try these methods:

✔ Press Enter to advance to the next cell down each row and then across each column in the range. Press Shift+Enter to move up to the previous cell.

✔ Press Tab to advance to the next cell in the column on the right and then down each row of the range. Press Shift+Tab to move left to the previous cell.

✔ Press Ctrl+. (period) to move from one corner of the range to another.

Data entry express

You can save a lot of time and energy when you want the same entry (text, value, or formula) to appear in many cells of the worksheet; you can enter the information in all the cells in one operation. You first select the cell ranges to hold the information. (Excel lets you select more than one cell range for this kind of thing — see Chapter 3 for details.) Then you construct the entry on the Formula bar and press Ctrl+Enter to put the entry into all the selected ranges.

The key to making this operation a success on a physical keyboard is to hold the Ctrl key down while you press Enter so that Excel inserts the entry on the Formula bar into all the selected cells. If you forget to hold Ctrl and you just press Enter, Excel places the entry in the first cell only of the selected cell range. On the Windows virtual keyboard, you just tap Ctrl followed by Enter in succession.

You can also speed up data entry in a list that includes formulas by making sure that the Extend Data Range Formats and Formulas check box is selected in the Editing Options section of the Advanced tab in the Excel Options dialog box. (Choose File⇨Options⇨Advanced or press Alt+FTA.) When this check box is selected, Excel automatically formats new data that you type in the last row of a list to match that of like data in earlier rows and copies formulas that appear in the preceding rows. Note, however, that for this new feature to kick in, you must manually enter the formulas and format the data entries in at least three rows preceding the new row.

How to Make Your Formulas Function Even Better

Instead of creating complex formulas from scratch out of an intricate combination of these operations, you can find an Excel function to get the job done.

A *function* is a predefined formula that performs a particular type of computation. All you have to do to use a function is supply the values that the function uses when performing its calculations. (In the parlance of the Spreadsheet Guru, such values are the *arguments of the function*.) As with simple formulas, you can enter the arguments for most functions either as a numerical value (for example, **22** or **–4.56**) or, as is more common, as a cell reference (**B10**) or as a cell range (**C3:F3**).

Just as with a formula you build yourself, each function you use must start with an equal sign (=) so that Excel knows to enter the function as a formula rather than as text. Following the equal sign, you enter the name of the function (in upper-case or lowercase — it doesn't matter, as long as you spell the name correctly). Following the name of the function, you enter the arguments required to perform the calculations. All function arguments are enclosed in a pair of parentheses.

If you type the function directly in a cell, remember not to insert spaces between the equal sign, function name, and the arguments enclosed in parentheses. Some functions use more than one value when performing their designated calculations. When this is the case, you separate each function with a comma (not a space).

After you type the equal sign and begin typing the first few letters of the name of the function you want to use, a drop-down list showing all the functions that begin with the letters you've typed appears immediately beneath the cell. When you see the name of the function you want to use on this list, double-click it and Excel finishes entering the function name in the cell and on the Formula bar as well as adding the left parenthesis that marks the beginning of the arguments for the function.

Excel then displays all the arguments that the function takes beneath the cell, and you can indicate any cell or cell range that you want to use as the first argument by either pointing to it or typing its cell or range references. When the function uses more than one argument, you can point to the cells or cell ranges or enter the addresses for the second argument right after you enter a comma (,) to complete the first argument.

After you finish entering the last argument, you need to close off the function by typing a right parenthesis to mark the end of the argument list. The display of the function name along with its arguments that appeared beneath the cell when you first selected the function from the drop-down list then disappears. Click the Enter button or press Enter (or the appropriate arrow key) to then insert the function into the cell and have Excel calculate the answer.

Inserting a function into a formula with the Insert Function button

Although you can enter a function by typing it directly in a cell, Excel provides an Insert Function command button on the Formula bar you can use to select any of Excel's functions. When you select this button, Excel opens the Insert Function dialog box (shown in Figure 2-14) where you can select the function you want to use. After you select your function, Excel opens the Function Arguments dialog box. In this dialog box, you can specify the function arguments. The real boon comes when you're starting to use an unfamiliar function or one that's kind of complex (some of these puppies can be hairy). You can get loads of help in completing the argument text boxes in the Function Arguments dialog box by clicking the Help on This Function link in the lower-left corner.

Figure 2-14: Select the function you want to use in the Insert Function dialog box.

The Insert Function dialog box contains three boxes: a Search for a Function text box, an Or Select a Category drop-down list box, and a Select a Function list box. When you open the Insert Function dialog box, Excel automatically selects Most Recently Used as the category in the Select a Category drop-down list box and displays the functions you usually use in the Select a Function list box.

If your function isn't among the most recently used, you must then select the appropriate category of your function in the

Select a Category drop-down list box. If you don't know the category, you must search for the function by typing a description of its purpose in the Search for a Function text box and then press Enter or click the Go button. For example, to locate all the Excel functions that total values, you enter **total** in the Search for a Function list box and click the Go button. Excel then displays its list of recommended functions for calculating totals in the Select a Function list box. You can peruse the recommended functions by selecting each one. While you select each function in this list, the Insert Function dialog box shows you the required arguments followed by a description, at the bottom of the dialog box, of what the function does.

After you locate and select the function that you want to use, click the OK button to insert the function into the current cell and open the Function Arguments dialog box. This dialog box displays the required arguments for the function along with any that are optional. For example, suppose that you select the SUM function (the crown jewel of the Most Recently Used function category) in the Select a Function list box and then select OK. As soon as you do, the program inserts

```
SUM( )
```

in the current cell and on the Formula bar (following the equal sign), and the Function Arguments dialog box showing the SUM arguments appears on the screen (as shown in Figure 2-15). This is where you add the arguments for the SUM function.

Figure 2-15: Specify the arguments to use in the selected function in the Function Arguments dialog box.

As shown in Figure 2-15, you can sum up to 255 numbers in the Function Arguments dialog box. What's not obvious, however (there's always some trick, huh?), is that these numbers don't have to be in single cells. In fact, most of the time you'll be selecting a whole slew of numbers in nearby cells (in a multiple cell selection — that range thing) that you want to total.

To select your first number argument in the dialog box, select the cell (or block of cells) in the worksheet while the insertion point is in the Number1 text box. Excel then displays the cell address (or range address) in the Number1 text box while, at the same time, showing the value in the cell (or values, if you select a bunch of cells) in the box to the right. Excel displays the total near the bottom of the Function Arguments dialog box after the words *Formula result=.*

When selecting cells, you can minimize this arguments dialog box to just the contents of the Number1 text box by dragging the cell pointer through the cells to sum in the worksheet. After you minimize the arguments dialog box while selecting the cells for the first argument, you can then expand it again by releasing the mouse button.

You can also reduce the dialog box to the Number1 argument text box by clicking the Minimize Dialog Box button on the right of the text box, selecting the cells, and then clicking the Maximize Dialog Box button (the only button displayed on the far right) or by pressing the Esc key. Instead of minimizing the dialog box, you can also temporarily move it out of the way by clicking on any part and then dragging the dialog box to its new destination on the screen.

If you're adding more than one cell (or a bunch of cells) in a worksheet, press the Tab key or click the Number2 text box to move the insertion point to that text box. (Excel responds by extending the argument list with a Number3 text box.) Here is where you specify the second cell (or cell range) to add to the one now showing in the Number1 text box. After you select the cell or second cell range, the program displays the cell address(es), the numbers in the cell(s) to the right, and the running total near the bottom of the Function Arguments dialog box after *Formula result=* (as shown in Figure 2-15). You can minimize the entire Function Arguments dialog box down to just the contents of the argument text box you're dealing with (Number2, Number3, and so on) by clicking its particular Minimize Dialog Box button if the dialog box obscures the cells that you need to select.

When you finish pointing out the cells or bunch of cells to sum, click the OK button to close the Function Arguments dialog box and put the SUM function in the current cell.

Editing a function with the Insert Function button

You can also use the Insert Function button to edit formulas that contain functions right from the Formula bar. Select the cell with the formula and function to edit before you select the Insert Function button (the one sporting the *fx* that appears immediately in front of the current cell entry on the Formula bar).

As soon as you select the Insert Function button, Excel opens the Function Arguments dialog box where you can edit its arguments. To edit just the arguments of a function, select the cell references in the appropriate argument's text box (marked Number1, Number2, Number3, and so on) and then make whatever changes are required to the cell addresses or select a new range of cells.

Excel automatically adds any cell or cell range that you high-light in the worksheet to the current argument. If you want to replace the current argument, you need to highlight it and remove its cell addresses by pressing the Delete key before you highlight the new cell or cell range to use as the argument. (Remember that you can always minimize this dialog box or move it to a new location if it obscures the cells you need to select.)

When you finish editing the function, press Enter or click the OK button in the Function Arguments dialog box to put it away and update the formula in the worksheet.

I'd be totally lost without AutoSum

Before leaving this fascinating discussion on entering functions, I want you to get to the AutoSum tool in the Editing group on the Home tab of the Ribbon. Look for the Greek sigma (Σ) symbol. This little tool is worth its weight in gold.

In addition to entering the SUM, AVERAGE, COUNT, MAX, or MIN functions, it also selects the most likely range of cells in the current column or row that you want to use as the function's argument and then automatically enters them as the function's argument. Nine times out of ten, Excel selects (with the *marquee* or moving dotted line) the correct cell range to total, average, count, and so forth. For that tenth case, you can manually correct the range by simply dragging the cell pointer through the block of cells to sum.

Simply select the AutoSum button followed by Sum on the drop-down menu on the Home tab when you want to insert the SUM function into the current cell. The quicker method to select this function is to press Alt+= (the Alt key plus the equal to symbol on the top row).

If you want to use the AutoSum button to insert another function, such as AVERAGE, COUNT, MAX, or MIN, you need to click its drop-down button and select the name of the desired function on its pop-up menu (click Count Numbers on the menu to insert the COUNT function). If you select the More Functions command on this menu, Excel opens the Insert Function dialog box as though you had clicked the *fx* button on the Formula bar.

In Figure 2-16, check out how to use AutoSum to total the sales of Jack Sprat Diet Centers in row 3. Position the cell pointer in cell E3 where the first-quarter total is to appear and then select Sum on the AutoSum drop-down menu (or press Alt+=). Excel inserts SUM (equal sign and all) onto the Formula bar; places a marquee around cells B3, C3, and D3; and uses the cell range B3:D3 as the argument of the SUM function.

Now look at the worksheet after you insert the function in cell E3 (see Figure 2-17). The calculated total appears in cell E3 while the following SUM function formula appears in the Formula bar:

```
=SUM(B3:D3)
```

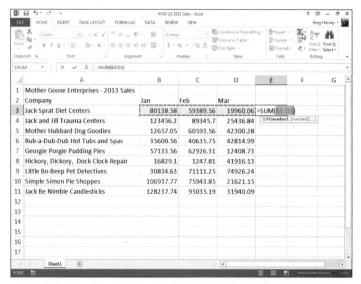

Figure 2-16: To total Jack Sprat Diet Centers first quarter sales for row 3, click the AutoSum button in cell E3 and then click Enter.

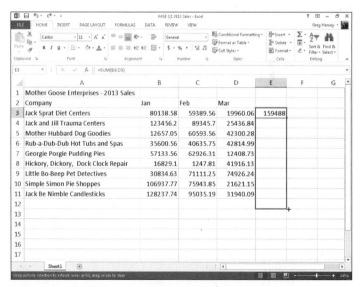

Figure 2-17: The worksheet with the first-quarter totals calculated with AutoSum.

After entering the function to total the sales of Jack Sprat Diet Centers, you can copy this formula to total sales for the rest of the companies by dragging the fill handle down column E until the cell range E3:E10 is highlighted (refer to Figure 2-17).

Look at Figure 2-18 to see how you can use AutoSum to total the January sales for all the Mother Goose Enterprises in column B. Position the cell pointer in cell B12 where you want the total to appear. Select Sum on the AutoSum's drop-down menu, and Excel places the marquee around cells B3 through B11 and correctly enters the cell range B3:B11 as the argument of the SUM function.

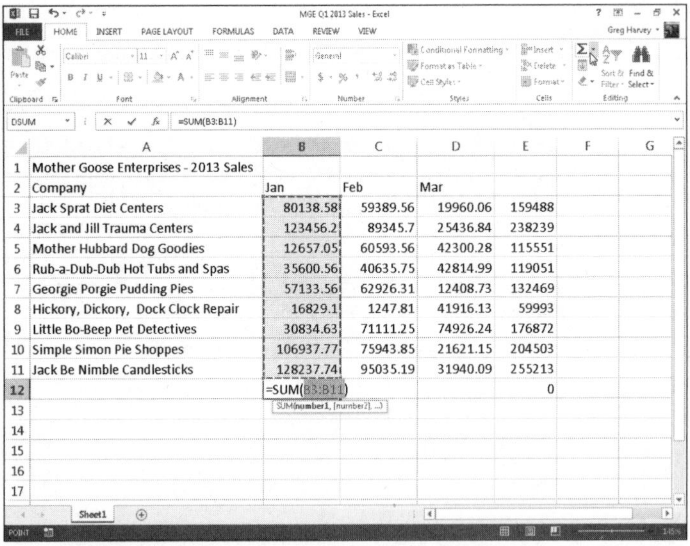

Figure 2-18: Select AutoSum in cell B12 and click Enter to total the January sales for all companies in column B.

In Figure 2-19, you see the worksheet after inserting the function in cell B12 and using the AutoFill feature to copy the formula to cells C12 and D12 to the right. (To use AutoFill, drag the fill handle through the cells to the right until you reach cell D12. Release the mouse button or remove your finger or stylus from the touchscreen.)

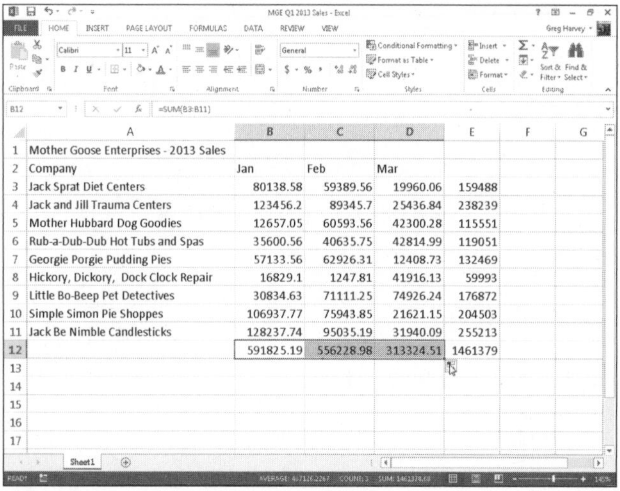

Figure 2-19: The worksheet after copying the SUM function formulas using the fill handle.

Sums via Quick Analysis Totals

For those of you who don't have the time or patience for adding totals to your worksheet tables with AutoSum and AutoFill, Excel 2013's Totals feature of the new Quick Analysis tool is just the thing. The Quick Analysis tool offers a bevy of features for doing anything from adding conditional formatting (see Chapter 3), charts, pivot tables, and sparklines to your worksheet tables. And it turns out Quick Analysis is also a whiz at adding running totals and sums to the rows and columns of your new worksheet tables.

To use the Quick Analysis tool, all you have to do is select the worksheet table's cells (see Chapter 3 for details) and then click the Quick Analysis tool that automatically appears in the lower-right corner of the last selected cell. When you do, a palette of options (from Formatting to Sparklines) appears right beneath the tool.

To add totals to your selected table data, simply click the Totals button. You can then use your mouse or Touch Pointer to have Live Preview show you totals in a new row at the bottom by highlighting Running Total or in a new column on the right by highlighting Sum (shown in Figure 2-20). To actually add the SUM formulas with the totals to a new row or column, simply click the Running Total or Sum button.

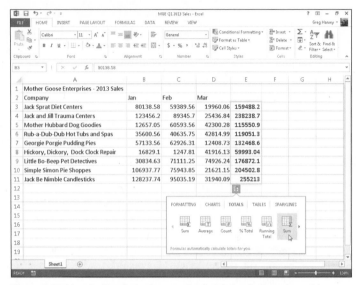

Figure 2-20: Use the Totals feature on the Quick Analysis tool to add a column of quarterly totals to a selected worksheet table.

To add the running totals to the sample worksheet table shown in Figure 2-20 after adding a column of quarterly totals with the Sum button, simply select the table of data, A2 through D12 (to include the new Sum column), and click the Quick Analysis tool followed by the Totals and Running Total buttons. Then, edit the heading, Sum, in cell E2 to make it read Qtr 1 and you're all done!

If you have trouble selecting the Quick Analysis tool to open its palette for any reason, simply right-click the cell selection and click the Quick Analysis item on its context menu.

Making Sure That the Data Is Safe and Sound

All the work you do in any of the worksheets in your workbook is at risk until you save the workbook as a disk file, normally on your computer's hard drive. Should you lose power or should your computer crash for any reason before you save the workbook, you're out of luck. You have to re-create each keystroke — a painful task made all the worse because it's so unnecessary. To avoid this unpleasantness altogether, adopt this motto: Save your work any time that you enter more information than you could possibly bear to lose.

To encourage frequent saving on your part, Excel even provides you with a Save button on the Quick Access toolbar (the one with the picture of a 3¼" floppy disk, the very first on the toolbar). You don't even have to take the time and trouble to choose the Save command from the File pull-down menu (opened by choosing File) or even press Ctrl+S; you can simply click this tool whenever you want to save new work on disk.

When you click the Save button, press Ctrl+S, or choose File⇨Save for the first time, Excel 2013 displays the Save As screen similar to the one shown in Figure 2-21. By default, Excel 2013 selects the Documents folder on your Windows Live SkyDrive as the place to save the new workbook.

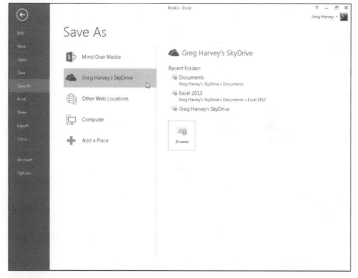

Figure 2-21: The Save As screen appears after you select the Save command to save a new workbook.

To save the file locally instead — on your computer's hard drive or a virtual drive on your local area network — click the Computer button under Windows Live's SkyDrive.

When you click Computer, the right pane of the Save As screen then displays a list of Recent Folders where you've recently saved Excel workbook files as well as any mapped network drives and your device's local Documents folder and Desktop. When you select the folder in this list into which you want to save the new workbook, Excel opens the Save As dialog box with the current contents of this folder displayed.

If none of the folders listed in the Computer pane of the Save As screen are where you want to save the workbook, go ahead and click the Browse button to open the Save As dialog box with the default location for saving workbook files from which you can select the drive and folder where the new workbook should be stored.

After the folder into which you want to save your new workbook is selected in the Save As dialog box, you then need to replace the temporary document name (Book1, Book2, and so forth) with a more descriptive filename in the File Name text box, select a new file format in the Save As Type drop-down list box, and select a new drive and folder before you save the workbook as a disk file.

When you finish making changes in the Save As dialog box, click the Save button or press Enter to have Excel 2013 save your work. When Excel saves your workbook file, the program saves all the information in every worksheet in your workbook (including the last position of the cell cursor) in the designated folder and drive.

You don't have to fool with the Save As dialog box again unless you want to rename the workbook or save a copy of it in a different folder. If you want to do these things, you must choose File➪Save As or press Alt+FA to choose the Save As command rather than clicking the Save button on the Quick Access toolbar or pressing Ctrl+S.

Changing the default file location

Whenever you open the Save As dialog box to save a new workbook file, Excel 2013 automatically selects the folder listed in the Default File Location text box on the Save tab of the Excel Options dialog box (File➪Options➪Save or Alt+FTS).

When you first start using Excel, the default folder is the Documents folder under your username on your hard drive.

For example, the directory path of the default folder where Excel 2013 automatically saves new workbook files on my computer is

```
C:\Users\Greg\Documents
```

The very generic Documents folder may not be the place on your hard drive where you want all the new workbooks you create automatically saved. To change the default file location to another folder on your computer, follow these steps:

1. **Choose File⇨Options⇨Save or press Alt+FTS to open the Save tab of the Excel Options dialog box.**

   The Default File Location text box displays the directory path to the current default folder.

2. **Click in the Default File Location text box.**

   To edit part of the path (such as the Documents folder name after your username), insert the mouse pointer at that place in the path to set the insertion point.

3. **Edit the existing path or replace it with the path to another folder in which you want all future workbooks to save to automatically.**

4. **Click OK to close the Excel Options dialog box.**

The difference between the XLSX and XLS file formats

Excel 2013 supports the use of the XML-based file format first introduced in Excel 2007 (which Microsoft officially calls the Microsoft Office Open XML format). This default file format is touted as being more efficient in saving data, resulting in smaller file size and offering superior integration with external data sources (especially when these resources are web-based ones supporting XML files). This XML-based file format carries the filename extension .xlsx and is the file format in which Excel automatically saves any new workbook you create.

The only problem with this newfangled XML-based file format is that it can't be opened by earlier Excel versions (before Excel 2007). Therefore, if someone who needs to work with the workbook you've just created isn't using Excel 2007 or hasn't yet upgraded to Excel 2013, you need to save the new workbook in the earlier file format used in Excel versions 97 through 2003 with the old `.xls` filename extension. To do this, click the Save As Type drop-down button in the Save As dialog box and then click Excel 97-2003 Workbook (*.xls) in the drop-down menu.

Filename extensions, such as `.xlsx` and `.xls`, do not appear as part of the filename (even though they are appended) in the File Name text box in the Excel Save As dialog box unless you've specifically changed Windows' folder options to show them. To make this change, open the Folder Options dialog box in Windows Explorer and then deselect the Hide Extensions for Known File Types check box on the View tab. To open the Folder Options dialog box in Windows 7 Explorer, click the Organize button and then select Folder and Search Options on its drop-down menu. To open this dialog box in Windows 8 Explorer, you select the View tab followed by the Options button on the Windows Explorer Ribbon.

Saving the Workbook as a PDF File

The PDF (Portable Document File) file format developed by Adobe Systems Incorporated enables people to open and print documents without access to the original programs with which the documents were created.

Excel 2013 enables you to save your workbook files directly in this special PDF file format. You can readily share your Excel 2013 workbooks with users who don't have Excel installed on their computers by saving them as PDF files. All they need to open and print the PDF copy of the workbook file is the free Adobe Reader software (which they can download from the Adobe website at www.adobe.com).

To save your workbook as a PDF file, simply select the PDF option on the Save as Type drop-down list in the Save As dialog box. Excel then adds PDF-specific options to the bottom of the Save As dialog box, with the Standard (Publishing Online and Printing) button under the Optimize For heading and the Open File after Publishing check box selected.

If you want to make the resulting PDF file as small as possible (because your worksheet is so large), click the Minimum Size (Publishing Online) button under the Optimize For heading. If you want to change which parts of the workbook are saved in the resulting PDF (Excel automatically saves all ranges in the active worksheet of the workbook), click the Options button directly beneath the Minimum Size (Publishing Online) option and make the appropriate changes in the Options dialog box before you click OK.

If you don't need to edit the filename (Excel automatically appends .pdf to the current filename) or the folder location in the Save As dialog box, simply click the Save button. Excel then saves a copy of the workbook in a PDF file format and, provided you don't deselect the Open File after Publishing check box, automatically opens the workbook for your inspection in Adobe Reader. After viewing the PDF version in Adobe Reader, you can then return to your worksheet in Excel by clicking the Reader's Close button (or pressing Alt+F4).

If you create an Excel 2013 workbook that incorporates new features not supported in earlier versions of Excel, instead of saving the workbook as an .xls file, thereby losing all of its 2010 enhancements, consider saving it as a PDF file. That way, co-workers still using pre-2010 Excel versions can still access the data in all its glory via Adobe Reader.

Document Recovery to the Rescue

Excel 2013 offers a document recovery feature that can help you in the event of a computer crash because of a power failure or some sort of operating system freeze or shutdown. The AutoRecover feature saves your workbooks at regular intervals. In the event of a computer crash, Excel displays a Document Recovery task pane the next time you start Excel after rebooting the computer.

When you first start using Excel 2013, the AutoRecover feature is set to automatically save changes to your workbook (provided that the file has already been saved) every ten minutes. You can shorten or lengthen this interval as you see fit. Choose File⇨ Options⇨Save or press Alt+FTS to open the Excel Options dialog box with the Save tab selected. Use the spinner buttons or enter a new automatic save interval into the text box marked Save AutoRecover Information Every 10 Minutes before clicking OK.

After re-launching Excel 2013 after a computer crash that prevents you from saving your workbook file, the program opens with the Document Recovery task pane on the left side of the screen. This Document Recovery task pane shows the available versions of the workbook files that were open at the time of the computer crash. The original version of the workbook file is identified, including when it was saved, as is the recovered version of the file (displaying an .xlsb file extension) and when it was saved.

To open the recovered version of a workbook (to see how much of the work it contains that was unsaved at the time of the crash), position the mouse pointer over the AutoRecover version, click its drop-down menu button followed by Open. After you open the recovered version, you can then (if you choose) save its changes by selecting the Save button on the Quick Access toolbar or by choosing File⇨Save.

To save the recovered version of a workbook without bothering to first open it, click the recovered version's drop-down button in the Document Recovery task pane, and then choose Save As. To abandon the recovered version permanently (leaving you with *only* the data in the original version), click the Close button at the bottom of the Document Recovery task pane. When you do this, an alert dialog box appears, giving you the chance to retain the recovered versions of the file for later viewing. To retain the files for later viewing, select the Yes (I Want to View These Files Later) radio button before clicking OK. To retain only the original versions of the files shown in the task pane, select the No (Remove These Files. I Have Saved the Files I Need) radio button instead.

The AutoRecover feature only works on Excel workbooks that you've saved at least one time (as explained in the earlier section "Making Sure That the Data Is Safe and Sound"). In other words, if you build a new workbook and don't bother to save and rename it prior to experiencing a computer crash, the AutoRecover feature will not bring back any part of it. For this reason, it is very important that you get into the habit of saving new workbooks with the Save button on the Quick Access toolbar very shortly after beginning to work on worksheets. Or use the trusty keyboard shortcut Ctrl+S.

Chapter 3

Making It All Look Pretty

*I*n spreadsheet programs like Excel, you normally don't worry about how the stuff looks until after you enter all the data in the worksheets of your workbook and save it all safe and sound (see Chapters 1 and 2). Only then do you pretty up the information so that it's clearer and easy to read.

After you decide on the types of formatting that you want to apply to a portion of the worksheet, you can select all the cells to beautify and then click the appropriate tool or choose the menu command to apply those formats to the cells. However, before you discover all the fabulous formatting features you can use to dress up cells, you need to know how to pick the group of cells that you want to apply the formatting to — that is, *selecting the cells* or, alternatively, *making a cell selection*.

Be aware, also, that entering data into a cell and formatting that data are two completely different things in Excel. Because they're separate, you can change the entry in a formatted cell, and new entries assume the cell's formatting. This enables you to format blank cells in a worksheet, knowing that when you get around to making entries in those cells, those entries automatically assume the formatting you assign to those cells.

Choosing a Select Group of Cells

A *cell selection* (or *cell range*) is whatever collection of neighboring cells you choose to format or edit. The smallest possible cell selection in a worksheet is just one cell: the so-called *active cell*. The cell with the cell cursor is really just a single cell selection. The largest possible cell selection in a worksheet is all the cells in that worksheet (the whole enchilada, so to speak). Most of the cell selections you need for formatting a worksheet will probably fall somewhere in between, consisting of cells in several adjacent columns and rows.

Excel shows a cell selection in the worksheet by highlighting in color the entire block of cells within the extended cell cursor, except for the active cell that keeps its original color. (Figure 3-1 shows several cell selections of different sizes and shapes.)

In Excel, you can select more than one cell range at a time (a phenomenon somewhat ingloriously called a *noncontiguous* or *nonadjacent selection*). In fact, although Figure 3-1 appears to contain several cell selections, it's really just one big, nonadjacent cell selection with cell D12 (the active one) as the cell that was selected last.

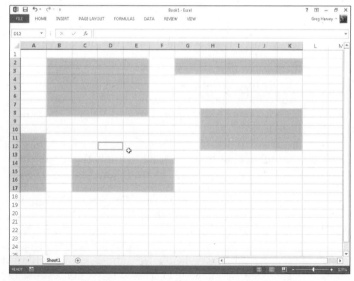

Figure 3-1: Several cell selections of various shapes and sizes.

Point-and-click cell selections

A mouse (provided that the device you're running Excel 2013 on has a mouse) is a natural for selecting a range of cells. Just position the mouse pointer (in its thick, white cross form) on the first cell and then click and drag in the direction that you want to extend the selection.

 ✔ To extend the cell selection to columns to the right, drag your mouse to the right, highlighting neighboring cells as you go.

 ✔ To extend the selection to rows to the bottom, drag your mouse down.

 ✔ To extend the selection down and to the right at the same time, drag your mouse diagonally toward the cell in the lower-right corner of the block you're highlighting.

Touchy-feely cell selections

If you're running Excel 2013 on a touchscreen device such as a Windows tablet or smartphone, simply use your finger or stylus to make your cell selections. Simply tap the first cell in the selection (the equivalent of clicking with a mouse) and then drag the selection handle (one of the two circles that appears in the upper-left and lower-right corner of the cell) through the rest of the adjacent cells to extend the cell selection and select the entire range.

Shifty cell selections

To speed up the old cell-selection procedure, you can use the Shift+click method, which goes as follows:

1. **Click the first cell in the selection.**

   This selects that cell.

2. **Position the mouse pointer in the last cell in the selection.**

   This is kitty-corner from the first cell in your selected rectangular block.

3. **Press the Shift key and hold it down while you click the mouse button again.**

   When you click the mouse button the second time, Excel selects all the cells in the columns and rows between the first cell and last cell.

The Shift key works with the mouse like an *extend* key to extend a selection from the first object you select through to, and including, the second object you select. See the section "Extend that cell selection," later in this chapter. Using the Shift key enables you to select the first and last cells, as well as all the intervening cells in a worksheet or all the document names in a list.

If, when making a cell selection with the mouse, you notice that you include the wrong cells before you release the mouse button, you can deselect the cells and resize the selection by moving the pointer in the opposite direction. If you already released the mouse button, click the first cell in the highlighted range to select just that cell (and deselect all the others) and then start the whole selection process again.

Nonadjacent cell selections

To select a nonadjacent cell selection made up of more than one non-touching block of cells, drag through the first cell range and release the mouse button. Then hold down the Ctrl key while you click the first cell of the second range and drag the pointer through the cells in this range. As long as you hold down Ctrl while you select the subsequent ranges, Excel doesn't deselect any of the previously selected cell ranges.

On your onscreen virtual keyboard, simply tap the Ctrl key to engage it — you don't have to keep it depressed as you do on a physical keyboard — before you go about dragging through the other cell selections. Just remember to tap the Ctrl key a second time to disengage when you're all done selecting your nonadjacent cells ranges.

The Ctrl key works with the mouse like an *add* key to include non-neighboring objects in Excel. See the section "Nonadjacent cell selections with the keyboard," later in this chapter. By using the Ctrl key, you can add to the selection of cells in a worksheet or to the document names in a list without having to deselect those already selected.

Going for the "big" cell selections

You can select the cells in entire columns or rows or even all the cells in the worksheet by applying the following clicking-and-dragging techniques to the worksheet frame:

- To select every single cell in a particular column, click its column letter on the frame at the top of the worksheet document window.

- To select every cell in a particular row, click its row number on the frame at the left edge of the document window.

- To select a range of entire columns or rows, drag through the column letters or row numbers on the frame surrounding the workbook.

- To select more than entire columns or rows that are not right next to each other (that old noncontiguous stuff, again), press and hold the Ctrl key while you click the column letters or row numbers of the columns or rows that you want to add to the selection.

- To select every cell in the worksheet, press Ctrl+A or click the Select All button, which is the button with the triangle pointing downward on the diagonal (which reminds me of the corner of a dog-eared book page). It's in the upper-left corner of the workbook frame, formed by the intersection of the row with the column letters and the column with the row numbers.

Selecting the cells in a table of data, courtesy of AutoSelect

Excel provides a quick way (called AutoSelect) to select all the cells in a table of data entered as a solid block. To use AutoSelect, simply follow these steps:

1. **Click the first cell of the table to select it.**

   This is the cell in the table's upper-left corner.

2. **Hold down the Shift key while you double-click the right or bottom edge of the selected cell with the arrowhead mouse pointer. (See Figure 3-2.)**

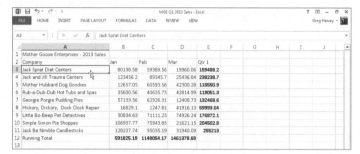

Figure 3-2: Position the mouse pointer on the first cell's bottom edge to select all cells of the table's first column.

Double-clicking the bottom edge of the cell causes the cell selection to expand to the cell in the last row of the first column (as shown in Figure 3-3). If you double-click the right edge of the cell, the cell selection expands to the cell in the last column of the first row.

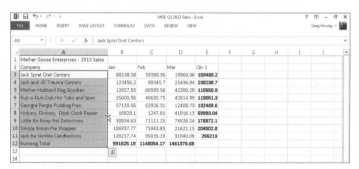

Figure 3-3: Hold down Shift while you double-click the bottom edge of the first cell to extend the selection down the column.

3a. Double-click somewhere on the right edge of the cell selection (refer to Figure 3-3) if the cell selection now consists of the first column of the table.

This selects all the remaining rows of the table of data (as shown in Figure 3-4).

3b. Double-click somewhere on the bottom edge of the current cell selection if the cell selection now consists of the first row of the table.

This selects all the remaining rows in the table.

Figure 3-4: Hold down Shift as you double-click the right edge of the current selection to extend it across the rows of the table.

Although the preceding steps may lead you to believe that you have to select the first cell of the table when you use AutoSelect, you can actually select any of the cells in the four corners of the table. Then, when expanding the cell selection in the table with the Shift key depressed, you can choose whatever direction you like to either select the first or last row of the table or the first or last column. (Choose left, by clicking the left edge; right, by clicking the right edge; up, by clicking the top edge; or down, by clicking the bottom edge.) After expanding the cell selection to include either the first or last row or first or last column, you need to click whichever edge of that current cell selection that will expand it to include all the remaining table rows or columns.

Keyboard cell selections

If you're not keen on using the mouse, you can use the keyboard to select the cells you want. Sticking with the Shift+click method of selecting cells, the easiest way to select cells with the keyboard is to combine the Shift key with other keystrokes that move the cell cursor. (I list these keystrokes in Chapter 1.)

Start by positioning the cell cursor in the first cell of the selection and then holding the Shift key while you press the appropriate cell-pointer movement keys. When you hold the Shift key while you press direction keys — such as the arrow keys ($\uparrow$, $\rightarrow$, $\downarrow$, $\leftarrow$), PgUp, or PgDn — Excel anchors the selection on the current cell, moves the cell cursor, and highlights cells as it goes.

When making a cell selection this way, you can continue to alter the size and shape of the cell range with the cell-pointer movement keys as long as you don't release the Shift key. After you release the Shift key, pressing any of the cell-pointer movement keys immediately collapses the selection, reducing it to just the cell with the cell cursor.

Extend that cell selection

If holding the Shift key while you move the cell cursor is too tiring, you can place Excel in Extend mode by pressing (and promptly releasing) F8 before you press any cell-pointer movement key. Excel displays the Extend Selection indicator on the left side of the Status bar — when you see this indicator, the program will select all the cells that you move the cell cursor through (just as though you were holding down the Shift key).

After you highlight all the cells you want in the cell range, press F8 again (or Esc) to turn off Extend mode. The Extend Selection indicator disappears from the status bar, and then you can once again move the cell cursor with the keyboard without highlighting everything in your path. In fact, when you first move the pointer, all previously selected cells are deselected.

AutoSelect keyboard style

For the keyboard equivalent of AutoSelect with the mouse (see the "Selecting the cells in a table of data, courtesy of AutoSelect" section), you combine the use of the F8 key (Extend key) or the Shift key with the Ctrl+arrow keys or End+arrow keys to zip the cell cursor from one end of a block to the other and merrily select all the cells in that path.

To select an entire table of data with a keyboard version of AutoSelect, follow these steps:

1. **Position the cell cursor in the first cell.**

   That's the cell in the upper-left corner of the table.

2. **Press F8 (or hold the Shift key) and then press Ctrl+→ to extend the cell selection to the cells in the columns on the right.**

3. **Then press Ctrl+↓ to extend the selection to the cells in the rows below.**

The directions in the preceding steps are somewhat arbitrary —
you can just as well press Ctrl+↓ before you press Ctrl+→.
Just be sure (if you're using the Shift key instead of F8) that
you don't let up on the Shift key until after you finish performing these two directional maneuvers. Also, if you press F8 to
get the program into Extend mode, don't forget to press this
key again to get out of Extend mode after the table cells are all
selected, or you'll end up selecting cells that you don't want
included when you next move the cell cursor.

Nonadjacent cell selections with the keyboard

Selecting more than one cell range is a little more complicated
with the keyboard than it is with the mouse. When using the
keyboard, you alternate between *anchoring* the cell cursor
and moving it to select the cell range and *unanchoring* the cell
cursor and repositioning it at the beginning of the next range.
To unanchor the cell cursor so that you can move it into position for selecting another range, press Shift+F8. This puts you
in Add to Selection mode, in which you can move to the first
cell of the next range without selecting any more cells. Excel
lets you know that the cell cursor is unanchored by displaying
the Add to Selection indicator on the left side of the Status bar.

To select more than one cell range by using the keyboard,
follow these general steps:

1. **Move the cell cursor to the first cell of the first cell
   range that you want to select.**

2. **Press F8 to get into Extend Selection mode.**

   Move the cell cursor to select all the cells in the first
   cell range. Alternatively, hold the Shift key while you
   move the cell cursor.

3. **Press Shift+F8 to switch from Extend Selection mode
   to Add to Selection mode.**

   The Add to Selection indicator appears in the Status bar.

4. **Move the cell cursor to the first cell of the next nonadjacent range that you want to select.**

5. **Press F8 again to get back into Extend Selection
   mode and then move the cell cursor to select all the
   cells in this new range.**

6. **If you still have other nonadjacent ranges to select, repeat Steps 3, 4, and 5 until you select and add all the cell ranges that you want to use.**

Cell selections à la Go To

If you want to select a large cell range that would take a long time to select by pressing various cell-pointer movement keys, use the Go To feature to extend the range to a far distant cell. All you gotta do is follow this pair of steps:

1. **Position the cell cursor in the first cell of the range and then press F8 to anchor the cell cursor and get Excel into Extend Selection mode.**

2. **Press F5 or Ctrl+G to open the Go To dialog box, type the address of the last cell in the range (the cell kitty-corner from the first cell), and then click OK or press Enter.**

Because Excel is in Extend Selection mode at the time you use the Go To feature to jump to another cell, the program not only moves the cell cursor to the designated cell address but selects all the intervening cells as well. After selecting the range of cells with the Go To feature, don't forget to press F8 (the Extend Selection key) again to prevent the program from messing up your selection by adding more cells the next time you move the cell cursor.

Using the Format as Table Gallery

Here's a formatting technique that doesn't require you to do any prior cell selecting. (Kinda figures, doesn't it?) The Format as Table feature is so automatic that the cell cursor just has to be within the table of data prior to you clicking the Format as Table command button in the Styles group on the Home tab. Clicking the Format as Table command button opens its rather extensive Table Styles gallery with the formatting thumbnails divided into three sections — Light, Medium, and Dark — each of which describes the intensity of the colors used by its various formats.

As soon as you click one of the table formatting thumbnails in this Table Styles gallery, Excel makes its best guess as to the cell range of the data table to apply it to (indicated by the marquee around its perimeter) and the Format As Table dialog box, similar to the one shown in Figure 3-5, appears.

	A	B	C	D	E	F	G	H	I	J	K
1	Production Schedule for 2014										
2											
3	Part No.	Apr-14	May-14	Jun-14	Jul-14	Aug-14	Sep-14	Oct-14	Nov-14	Dec-14	
4	Part 100	500	485	438	505	483	540	441	550	345	
5	Part 101	175	170	153	177	169	189	154	193	200	
6	Part 102	350	340	306	354	338	378	309	385	350	
7	Part 103	890	863	779	899	859	961	785	979	885	
8	Total	1915	1858	1676	1934	1848	2068	1689	2107	1780	

Figure 3-5: Selecting a format from the Table Styles gallery and indicating its range in the Format As Table dialog box.

This dialog box contains a Where Is the Data for Your Table text box that shows the address of the cell range currently selected by the marquee and a My Table Has Headers check box.

If Excel does not correctly guess the range of the data table you want to format, drag through the cell range to adjust the marquee and the range address in the Where Is the Data for Your Table text box. If your data table doesn't use column headers or, if the table has them, but you still don't want Excel to add Filter drop-down buttons to each column heading, deselect the My Table Has Headers check box before you click the OK button.

WARNING! The table formats in the Table Styles gallery are not available if you select multiple nonadjacent cells before you click the Format as Table command button on the Home tab.

After you click the OK button in the Format As Table dialog box, Excel applies the formatting of the thumbnail you clicked in the gallery to the data table. Additionally, the Design tab appears under the Table Tools contextual tab at the end of the Ribbon, and the table is selected with the Quick Analysis tool appearing in the lower-right corner, as shown in Figure 3-6.

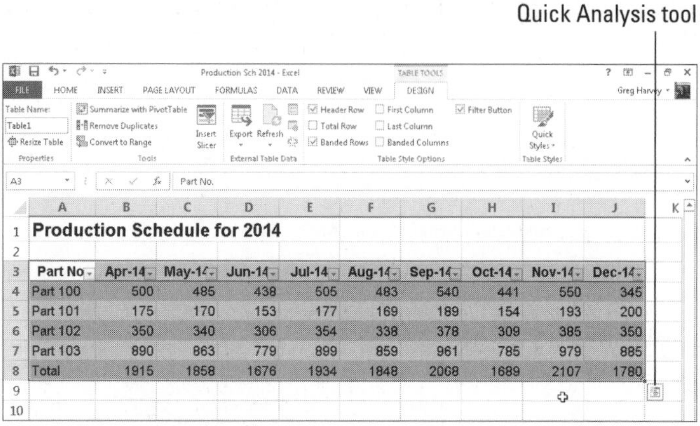

Quick Analysis tool

Figure 3-6: After you select a format from the Table Styles gallery, the Design tab appears under the Table Tools contextual tab.

The Design tab enables you to use Live Preview to see how your table would appear. Simply click the Quick Styles button on the Ribbon and then position the mouse or Touch Pointer over any of the format thumbnails in the Table Styles group to see the data in your table appear in that table format. Click the button with the triangle pointing downward to scroll up new rows of table formats in the Table Styles group; click the button with the triangle pointing upward to scroll down rows without opening the Table Styles gallery and possibly obscuring the actual data table in the Worksheet area. Click the More button (the one with the horizontal bar above the downward-pointing triangle) to redisplay the Table gallery and then mouse over the thumbnails in the Light, Medium, and Dark sections to have Live Preview apply them to the table.

In addition to enabling you to select a new format from the Table Styles gallery, the Design tab contains a Table Style Options group containing a bunch of check boxes that enable you to customize the look of the selected table format even further:

✔ **Header Row** to add special formatting and Filter buttons to each of the column headings in the first row of the table.

✔ **Total Row** to have Excel add a Total Row to the bottom of the table that displays the sums of each column that contains values. To apply another Statistical function to the values in a particular column, click the cell in that column's Total Row to display a drop-down list button and then select the function — Average, Count, Count Numbers, Max, Min, Sum, StdDev (Standard Deviation), or Var (Variance).

✔ **Banded Rows** to have Excel apply shading to every other row in the table.

✔ **First Column** to have Excel display the row headings in the first column of the table in bold.

✔ **Last Column** to have Excel display the row headings in the last column of the table in bold.

✔ **Banded Columns** to have Excel apply shading to every other column in the table.

Whenever you assign a format in the Table Styles gallery to one of the data tables in your workbook, Excel automatically assigns that table a generic range name (Table1, Table2, and so on). You can use the Table Name text box in the Properties group on the Design tab to rename the data table to give it a more descriptive range name.

When you finish selecting and/or customizing the formatting of your data table, click a cell outside of the table to remove the Table Tools contextual tab (with its Design tab) from the Ribbon. If later, you decide that you want to further experiment with the table's formatting, click any of the table's cells to redisplay the Table Tools' Design tab at the end of the Ribbon.

You can also use the Tables option on the Quick Analysis tool to format your worksheet data as a table. Simply select the table data (including headings) as a cell range in the worksheet and then click the Tables option on the Quick Analysis tool, followed by the Table option below at the very beginning of the Tables' options. Excel then assigns the Table Style Medium 2 style to your table while at same time selecting the Design tab on the Ribbon. Then if you're not too keen on this table style, you can use Live Preview in the Tables Styles gallery on this tab to find the table formatting that you do want to use.

Cell Formatting from the Home Tab

Some spreadsheet tables or ranges within them require a lighter touch than the Format as Table command button offers. For example, you may have a data table where the only emphasis you want to add is to make the column headings bold at the top of the table and to underline the row of totals at the bottom (done by drawing a borderline along the bottom of the cells).

The formatting buttons that appear in the Font, Alignment, and Number groups on the Home tab enable you to accomplish just this kind of targeted cell formatting. See Table 3-1 for a complete rundown on how to use each of these formatting buttons.

Table 3-1   Formatting Command Buttons in the Font, Alignment, and Number Groups on the Home Tab

Group	Button Name	Function
Font		
	Font	Displays a Font drop-down menu from which you can select a new font for your cell selection
	Font Size	Displays a Font Size drop-down menu from which you can select a new font size for your cell selection — click the Font Size text box and enter the desired point size if it doesn't appear on the drop-down menu
	Increase Font Size	Increases the size of the font in the cell selection by one point
	Decrease Font Size	Decreases the size of the font in the cell selection by one point
	Bold	Applies boldface to the entries in the cell selection
	Italic	Italicizes the entries in the cell selection

Group	Button Name	Function
Font		
	Underline	Underlines the entries in the cell selection
	Borders	Displays a Borders drop-down menu from which you can select a border style for the cell selection
	Fill Color	Displays a Color drop-down palette from which you can select a new background color for the cell selection
	Font Color	Displays a Color drop-down palette from which you can select a new font color for the cell selection
Alignment		
	Align Left	Aligns all the entries in the cell selection with the left edge of their cells
	Center	Centers all the entries in the cell selection within their cells
	Align Right	Aligns all the entries in the cell selection with the right edge of their cells
	Decrease Indent	Decreases the margin between entries in the cell selection and their left cell borders by one tab stop
	Increase Indent	Increases the margin between the entries in the cell selection and their left cell borders by one tab stop
	Top Align	Aligns the entries in the cell selection with the top border of their cells
	Middle Align	Vertically centers the entries in the cell selection between the top and bottom borders of their cells
	Bottom Align	Aligns the entries in the cell selection with the bottom border of their cells
	Orientation	Displays a drop-down menu with options for changing the angle and direction of the entries in the cell selection
	Wrap Text	Wraps the entries in the cell selection that spill over their right borders onto multiple lines within the current column width

(continued)

Table 3-1 *(continued)*

Group	Button Name	Function
Alignment		
	Merge and Center	Merges the cell selection into a single cell and then centers the entry in the first cell between its new left and right border — click the Merge and Center drop-down button to display a menu of options that enable you to merge the cell selection into a single cell without centering the entries, as well as to split up a merged cell back into its original individual cells
Number		
	Number Format	Displays the number format applied to the active cell in the cell selection — click its drop-down button to display a menu showing the active cell in cell selection formatted with all of Excel's major number formats
	Accounting Number Format	Formats the cell selection using the Accounting number format that adds a dollar sign, uses commas to separate thousands, displays two decimal places, and encloses negative values in a closed pair of parentheses — click the Accounting Number Format's drop-down button to display a menu of other major Currency number formats from which you can choose
	Percent Style	Formats the cell selection using the Percentage number format that multiplies the values by 100 and adds a percent sign with no decimal places
	Comma Style	Formats the cell selection with the Comma Style number format that uses commas to separate thousands, displays two decimal places, and encloses negative values in a closed pair of parentheses

Group	Button Name	Function
Alignment		
	Increase Decimal	Adds a decimal place to the values in the cell selection
	Decrease Decimal	Removes a decimal place from the values in the cell selection

Don't forget about the tooltips that appear when you highlight one of these formatting command buttons with your mouse or Touch Pointer. These tooltips not only give you a short description of the button's function, but also display any shortcut keys for quickly adding or removing attributes from the entries in the cell selection.

Formatting Cells Close to the Source with the Mini-bar

Excel 2013 makes it easy to apply common formatting changes to a cell selection right within the Worksheet area thanks to the mini-toolbar feature, nicknamed the mini-bar (makes me thirsty just thinking about it!).

To display the mini-bar, select the cells that need formatting and then right-click somewhere in the cell selection. The cell range's context menu along with the mini-bar then appears to the right of the cell selection. When you select a tool in the mini-bar such the Font or Font Size pop-up button, the context menu disappears (see Figure 3-7).

As you can see in this figure, the mini-bar contains most of the buttons from the Font group of the Home tab (with the exception of the Underline button). It also contains the Center and Merge & Center buttons from the Alignment group (see the "Altering the Alignment" section, later in this chapter) and the Accounting Number Format, Percent Style, Comma Style, Increase Decimal, and Decrease Decimal buttons from the Number group (see the "Understanding the number formats" section, later in this chapter). Simply click these buttons to apply their formatting to the current cell selection.

Context menu

Mini-bar

Figure 3-7: Use the buttons on the mini-bar to apply common formatting changes to the cell selection within the Worksheet area.

Additionally, the mini-bar contains the Format Painter button from the Clipboard group of the Home tab that you can use to copy the formatting in the active cell to a cell selection you make (see the "Fooling Around with the Format Painter" section, later in this chapter for details).

Using the Format Cells Dialog Box

Although the command buttons in the Font, Alignment, and Number groups on the Home tab give you immediate access to the most commonly used formatting commands, they do not represent all of Excel's formatting commands by any stretch of the imagination.

To have access to all the formatting commands, you need to open the Format Cells dialog box by doing any of the following:

✔ Click the More Number Formats option at the very bottom of the drop-down menu attached to the Number Format button

✔ Click the Number Format dialog box launcher in the lower right of the Number group

✔ Press Ctrl+1

The Format Cells dialog box that this command calls up contains six tabs: Number, Alignment, Font, Border, Fill, and Protection. In this chapter, I show you how to use them all except the Protection tab.

The keystroke shortcut that opens the Format Cells dialog box — Ctrl+1 — is one worth knowing. Just press the Ctrl key plus the *number* 1 key, and not the *function key* F1.

Understanding the number formats

As I explain in Chapter 2, how you enter values into a worksheet determines the type of number format that they get. Here are some examples:

✔ If you enter a financial value complete with the dollar sign and two decimal places, Excel assigns a Currency number format to the cell along with the entry.

✔ If you enter a value representing a percentage as a whole number followed by the percent sign without any decimal places, Excel assigns the cell the Percentage number format that follows this pattern along with the entry.

✔ If you enter a date (dates are values, too) that follows one of the built-in Excel number formats, such as 11/06/13 or 06-Nov-13, the program assigns a Date number format that follows the pattern of the date along with a special value representing the date.

Although you can format values in this manner as you go along (which is necessary in the case of dates), you don't have to do it this way. You can always assign a number format to a group of values before or after you enter them. Formatting numbers after you enter them is often the most efficient way to go because it's just a two-step procedure:

1. **Select all the cells containing the values that need dressing up.**

2. **Select the number format that you want to use from the formatting command buttons on the Home tab or the options available on the Number tab in the Format Cells dialog box.**

Even if you're a really, really good typist and prefer to enter each value exactly as you want it to appear in the worksheet, you still have to resort to using number formats to make the values that are calculated by formulas match the others you enter. This is because Excel applies a General number format (which the Format Cells dialog box defines: "General format cells have no specific number format.") to all the values it calculates, as well as any you enter that don't exactly follow one of the other Excel number formats. The biggest problem with the General format is that it has the nasty habit of dropping all leading and trailing zeros from the entries. This makes it very hard to line up numbers in a column on their decimal points.

You can view this sad state of affairs in Figure 3-8, which is a sample worksheet with the first-quarter 2013 sales figures for Mother Goose Enterprises before any of the values have been formatted. Notice how the decimal in the numbers in the monthly sales figures columns zig and zag because they aren't aligned on the decimal place. This is the fault of Excel's General number format; the only cure is to format the values with a uniform number format.

	A	B	C	D	E	F	G	H
1	Mother Goose Enterprises - 2013 Sales							
2		Jan	Feb	Mar	Qtr 1			
3	Jack Sprat Diet Centers	80138.58	59389.56	19960.06	159488.2			
4	Jack and Jill Trauma Centers	12345.62	89645.57	25436.84	127428.03			
5	Mother Hubbard Dog Goodies	12657.05	60593.56	42300.28	115550.89			
6	Rub-a-Dub-Dub Hot Tubs and Spas	17619.79	406.35	42814.99	60841.13			
7	Georgie Porgie Pudding Pies	57133.56	62926.31	12408.75	132468.62			
8	Hickory, Dickory, Dock Clock Repair	1685.91	124718.1	4916.13	131320.14			
9	Little Bo-Beep Pet Detectives	30834.63	71111.25	74926.24	176872.12			
10	Running Total	212415.14	468790.7	222763.29	903969.13			
11								
12	Monthly/Qtrly Percentage	0.2349805	0.5185915	0.246428				
13								
14								

Figure 3-8: Numbers with decimals don't align when you choose General formatting.

Accounting for the dollars and cents in your cells

Given the financial nature of most worksheets, you probably use the Accounting number format more than any other. Applying this format is easy because you can assign it to the cell selection simply by clicking the Accounting Number Format button on the Home tab.

The Accounting number format adds a dollar sign, commas between thousands of dollars, and two decimal places to any values in a selected range. If any of the values in the cell selection are negative, this number format displays them in parentheses (the way accountants like them). If you want a minus sign in front of your negative financial values rather than enclosing them in parentheses, select the Currency format on the Number Format drop-down menu or on the Number tab of the Format Cells dialog box.

You can see in Figure 3-9 that only the cells containing totals are selected (cell ranges E3:E10 and B10:D10). This cell selection was then formatted with the Accounting number format by simply clicking its command button (the one with the $ icon, naturally) in the Number group on the Ribbon's Home tab.

	A	B	C	D	E	F	G
1	Mother Goose Enterprises - 2013 Sales						
2		Jan	Feb	Mar	Qtr 1		
3	Jack Sprat Diet Centers	80138.58	59389.56	19960.06	$159,488.20		
4	Jack and Jill Trauma Centers	12345.62	89645.57	25436.84	$127,428.03		
5	Mother Hubbard Dog Goodies	12657.05	60593.56	42300.28	$115,550.89		
6	Rub-a-Dub-Dub Hot Tubs and Spas	17619.79	406.35	42814.99	$ 60,841.13		
7	Georgie Porgie Pudding Pies	57133.56	62926.31	12408.75	$132,468.62		
8	Hickory, Dickory, Dock Clock Repair	1685.91	124718.1	4916.13	$131,320.14		
9	Little Bo-Beep Pet Detectives	30834.63	71111.25	74926.24	$176,872.12		
10	Running Total	$212,415.14	$468,790.70	$222,763.29	$903,969.13		
11							
12	Monthly/Qtrly Percentage	0.234980524	0.518591492	0.246427984			
13							
14							
15							

Figure 3-9: The totals in the Mother Goose sales table after clicking the Accounting Number Format button on the Home tab.

Although you could put all the figures in the table into the Accounting number format to line up the decimal points, this would result in a superabundance of dollar signs in a fairly small table. In this example, I only formatted the monthly and quarterly totals with the Accounting number format.

"Look, Ma, no more format overflow!"

When I apply the Accounting number format to the selection in the cell ranges of E3:E10 and B10:D10 in the sales table shown in Figure 3-9, Excel adds dollar signs, commas between the thousands, a decimal point, and two decimal places to the highlighted values. At the same time, Excel automatically widens columns B, C, D, and E just enough to display all this new formatting. In versions of Excel earlier than Excel 2003, you had to widen these columns yourself, and instead of the perfectly aligned numbers, you were confronted with columns of #######s in cell ranges E3:E10 and B10:D10. Such pound signs (where nicely formatted dollar totals should be) serve as overflow indicators, declaring that whatever formatting you added to the value in that cell has added so much to the value's display that Excel can no longer display it within the current column width.

Fortunately, Excel eliminates the format overflow indicators when you're formatting the values in your cells by automatically widening the columns. The only time you'll ever run across these dreaded #######s in your cells is when you take it upon yourself to narrow a worksheet column manually (see the section "Calibrating Columns," later in this chapter) to the extent that Excel can no longer display all the characters in its cells with formatted values.

Currying your cells with the Comma Style

The Comma Style format offers a good alternative to the Currency format. Like Currency, the Comma Style format inserts commas in larger numbers to separate thousands, hundred thousands, millions, and . . . well, you get the idea.

This format also displays two decimal places and puts negative values in parentheses. What it doesn't display is dollar signs. This makes it perfect for formatting tables where it's obvious that you're dealing with dollars and cents or for larger values that have nothing to do with money.

The Comma Style format also works well for the bulk of the values in the sample first-quarter sales worksheet. Check out Figure 3-10 to see this table after I format the cells containing the monthly sales for all the Mother Goose Enterprises with the Comma Style format. To do this, select the cell range B3:D9 and click the Comma Style button — the one with the comma icon (,) — in the Number group on the Home tab.

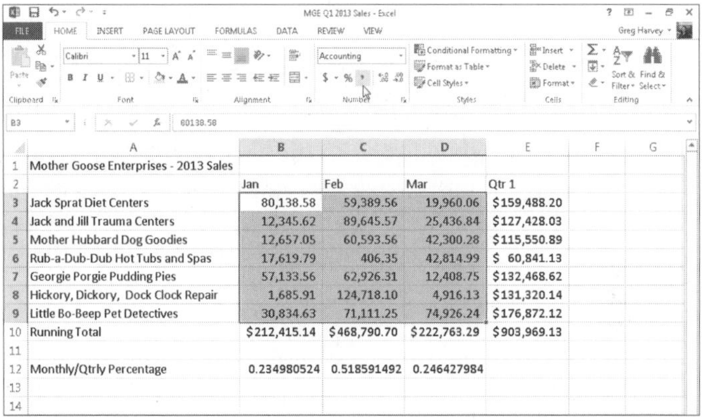

	A	B	C	D	E
1	Mother Goose Enterprises - 2013 Sales				
2		Jan	Feb	Mar	Qtr 1
3	Jack Sprat Diet Centers	80,138.58	59,389.56	19,960.06	$159,488.20
4	Jack and Jill Trauma Centers	12,345.62	89,645.57	25,436.84	$127,428.03
5	Mother Hubbard Dog Goodies	12,657.05	60,593.56	42,300.28	$115,550.89
6	Rub-a-Dub-Dub Hot Tubs and Spas	17,619.79	406.35	42,814.99	$ 60,841.13
7	Georgie Porgie Pudding Pies	57,133.56	62,926.31	12,408.75	$132,468.62
8	Hickory, Dickory, Dock Clock Repair	1,685.91	124,718.10	4,916.13	$131,320.14
9	Little Bo-Beep Pet Detectives	30,834.63	71,111.25	74,926.24	$176,872.12
10	Running Total	$212,415.14	$468,790.70	$222,763.29	$903,969.13
11					
12	Monthly/Qtrly Percentage	0.234980524	0.518591492	0.246427984	
13					
14					

Figure 3-10: Monthly sales figures after formatting cells with the Comma Style number format.

Note how, in Figure 3-10, the Comma Style format takes care of the earlier decimal alignment problem in the quarterly sales figures. Moreover, Comma Style–formatted monthly sales figures align perfectly with the Currency format–styled monthly totals in row 10. If you look closely (you may need a magnifying glass for this one), you see that these formatted values no longer abut the right edges of their cells; they've moved slightly to the left. The gap on the right between the last digit and the cell border accommodates the right parenthesis in negative values, ensuring that they, too, align precisely on the decimal point.

Playing around with Percent Style

Many worksheets use percentages in the form of interest rates, growth rates, inflation rates, and so on. To insert a percentage in a cell, type the percent sign (%) after the number. To indicate an interest rate of 12 percent, for example, you enter **12%** in the cell. When you do this, Excel assigns a Percentage number format and, at the same time, divides the value by 100 (that's what makes it a percentage) and places the result in the cell (0.12 in this example).

Not all percentages in a worksheet are entered by hand in this manner. Some may be calculated by a formula and returned to their cells as raw decimal values. In such cases, you should add a Percent format to convert the calculated decimal values to percentages (done by multiplying the decimal value by 100 and adding a percent sign).

The sample first-quarter-sales worksheet just happens to have some percentages calculated by formulas in row 12 that need formatting (these formulas indicate what percentage each monthly total is of the first-quarter total in cell E10). In Figure 3-11, these values reflect Percent Style formatting. To accomplish this feat, you simply select the cells and click the Percent Style button in the Number group on the Home tab.

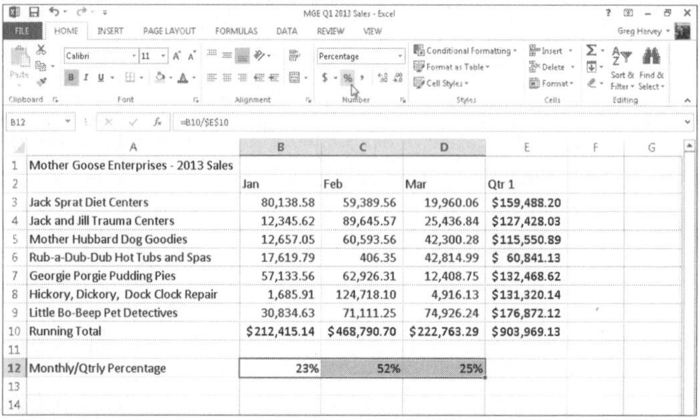

Figure 3-11: Monthly-to-quarterly sales percentages with Percentage number formatting.

Deciding how many decimal places

You can increase or decrease the number of decimal places used in a number entered by using the Accounting Number Format, Comma Style, or Percent Style button in the Number group of the Home tab simply by clicking the Increase Decimal button or the Decrease Decimal button in this group. Each time you click the Increase Decimal button (the one with the arrow pointing left), Excel adds another decimal place to the number format you apply.

The values behind the formatting

Make no mistake about it — all that these fancy number formats do is spiff up the presentation of the values in the worksheet. Like a good illusionist, a particular number format sometimes appears to transform some entries, but in reality, the entries are the same old numbers you started with. For example, suppose that a formula returns the following value:

```
25.6456
```

Now suppose that you format the cell containing this value with the Accounting Number Format button on the Home tab. The value now appears as follows:

```
$25.65
```

This change may lead you to believe that Excel rounded the value up to two decimal places. In fact, the program has rounded up only the *display* of the calculated value — the cell still contains the same old value of 25.6456. If you use this cell in another worksheet formula, Excel uses the behind-the-scenes value in its calculation, not the spiffed-up one shown in the cell.

If you want the values to match their formatted appearance in the worksheet, Excel can do that in a single step. Be forewarned, however, that this is a one-way trip. You can convert all underlying values to the way they are displayed by selecting a single check box, but you can't return them to their previous state by deselecting this check box.

Well, because you insist on knowing this little trick anyway, here goes (just don't write and try to tell me that you weren't warned):

1. **Make sure that you format all the values in your worksheet with the correct number of decimal places.**

   You must do this step before you convert the precision of all values in the worksheet to their displayed form.

2. **Choose File⇨Options⇨Advanced or press Alt+FTA to open the Advanced tab of the Excel Options dialog box.**

3. **In the When Calculating This Workbook section, click the Set Precision as Displayed check box (to fill it with a check mark).**

   Excel displays the Data Will Permanently Lose Accuracy alert dialog box.

4. **Go ahead (live dangerously) and click the OK button or press Enter to convert all values to match their display. Click OK again to close the Excel Options dialog box.**

Save the workbook with the calculated values. After converting all the values in a worksheet by selecting the Set Precision as Displayed check box, open the Save As dialog box (File⇨Save As or press Alt+FA). Edit the filename in the File Name text box (maybe by appending **as Displayed** to the current file-name) before you click the Save button or press Enter. That way, you'll have two copies: the original workbook file with the values as entered and calculated by Excel and the new *as Displayed* version.

Make it a date!

In Chapter 2, I mention that you can easily create formulas that calculate the differences between the dates and times that you enter in your worksheets. The only problem is that when Excel subtracts one date from another date or one time from another time, the program automatically formats the calculated result in a corresponding date or time number format as well. For example, if you enter 8-15-12 in cell B4 and 4/15/12 in cell C4 and in cell D4 enter the following formula for finding the number of elapsed days between the two dates:

```
=B4-C4
```

Excel correctly returns the result of 122 (days) using the General number format. However, when dealing with formulas that calculate the difference between two times in a work-sheet, you have to reformat the result that appears in a cor-responding time format into the General format. For example, suppose that you enter 8:00 AM in cell B5 and 4:00 PM in cell C5 and then create in cell D5 the following formula for calcu-lating the difference in hours between the two times:

```
=C5-B5
```

You then have to convert the result in cell D5 — that automatically appears as 8:00 AM — to the General format. When you do this, the fraction 0.333333 — representing its fraction of the total 24-hour period — replaces 8:00 AM in cell D5. You can then convert this fraction of a total day into the corresponding number of hours by multiplying this cell by 24 and formatting the cell with the General format.

Ogling some of the other number formats

Excel supports more number formats than just the Accounting, Comma Style, and Percentage number formats. To use them, select the cell range (or ranges) you want to format and select Format Cells on the cell shortcut menu (right-click somewhere in the cell selection to activate this menu) or just press Ctrl+1 to open the Format Cells dialog box.

After the Format Cells dialog box opens with the Number tab displayed, you select the desired format from the Category list box. Some number formats — such as Date, Time, Fraction, and Special — give you further formatting choices in a Type list box. Other number formats, such as Number and Currency, have their own particular boxes that give you options for refining their formats. When you click the different formats in these list boxes, Excel shows what effect this would have on the first of the values in the current cell selection in the Sample area above. When the sample has the format that you want to apply to the current cell selection, you just click OK or press Enter to apply the new number format.

Excel contains a nifty category of number formats called Special. The Special category contains the following four number formats that may interest you:

 ✔ **Zip Code:** Retains any leading zeros in the value (important for zip codes and of absolutely no importance in arithmetic computations). Example: 00123.

 ✔ **Zip Code + 4:** Automatically separates the last four digits from the first five digits and retains any leading zeros. Example: 00123-5555.

✔ **Phone Number:** Automatically encloses the first three digits of the number in parentheses and separates the last four digits from the previous three with a dash. Example: (999) 555-1111.

✔ **Social Security Number:** Automatically puts dashes in the value to separate its digits into groups of three, two, and four. Example: 666-00-9999.

These Special number formats really come in handy when creating data lists in Excel that often deal with stuff like zip codes, telephone numbers, and sometimes even Social Security numbers.

Calibrating Columns

For those times when Excel 2013 doesn't automatically adjust the width of your columns to your complete satisfaction, the program makes changing the column widths a breeze. The easiest way to adjust a column is to do a *best-fit,* using the AutoFit feature. With this method, Excel automatically determines how much to widen or narrow the column to fit the longest entry currently in the column.

Here's how to use AutoFit to get the best fit for a column:

1. **Position the mouse or Touch Pointer on the right border of the worksheet frame with the column letter at the top of the worksheet.**

   The pointer changes to a double-headed arrow pointing left and right.

2. **Double-click the mouse button.**

   Excel widens or narrows the column width to suit the longest entry.

You can apply a best-fit to more than one column at a time. Simply select all the columns that need adjusting (if the columns neighbor one another, drag through their column letters on the frame; if they don't, hold down the Ctrl key while you click the individual column letters). After you select the columns, double-click any of the right borders on the frame.

Best-fit à la AutoFit doesn't always produce the expected results. A long title that spills into several columns to the right produces a very wide column when you use best-fit.

When AutoFit's best-fit won't do, drag the right border of the column (on the frame) until it's the size you need instead of double-clicking it. This manual technique for calibrating the column width also works when more than one column is selected. Just be aware that all selected columns assume whatever size you make the one that you're actually dragging.

You can also set the widths of columns from the Format button's drop-down list in the Cells group on the Home tab. When you click this drop-down button, the Cell Size section of this drop-down menu contains the following width options:

✔ **Column Width** to open the Column Width dialog box where you enter the number of characters that you want for the column width before you click OK

✔ **AutoFit Column Width** to have Excel apply best-fit to the columns based on the widest entries in the current cell selection

✔ **Default Width** to open the Standard Width dialog box containing the standard column width of 8.43 characters that you can apply to the columns in the cell selection

Rambling rows

The story with adjusting the heights of rows is pretty much the same as that with adjusting columns except that you do a lot less row adjusting than you do column adjusting. That's because Excel automatically changes the height of the rows to accommodate changes to their entries, such as selecting a larger font size or wrapping text in a cell. I discuss both of these techniques in the upcoming section "Altering the Alignment." Most row-height adjustments come about when you want to increase the amount of space between a table title and the table or between a row of column headings and the table of information without actually adding a blank row. (See the section "From top to bottom," later in this chapter, for details.)

To increase the height of a row, drag the bottom border of the row frame down until the row is high enough and then release the mouse button. To shorten a row, reverse this process and drag the bottom row-frame border up. To use AutoFit to best-fit the entries in a row, double-click the bottom row-frame border.

As with columns, you can also adjust the height of selected rows using row options in the Cell Size section on the Format button's drop-down menu on the Home tab:

- ✓ **Row Height** to open the Row Height dialog box where you enter the number of points in the Row Height text box and then click OK

- ✓ **AutoFit Row Height** to return the height of selected rows to the best fit

Now you see it, now you don't

A funny thing about narrowing columns and rows: You can get carried away and make a column so narrow or a row so short that it actually disappears from the worksheet! This can come in handy for those times when you don't want part of the worksheet visible. For example, suppose you have a worksheet that contains a column listing employee salaries — you need these figures to calculate the departmental budget figures, but you would prefer to leave sensitive info off most printed reports. Rather than waste time moving the column of salary figures outside the area to be printed, you can just hide the column until after you print the report.

Hiding worksheet columns

Although you can hide worksheet columns and rows by just adjusting them out of existence, Excel does offer an easier method of hiding them, via the Hide & Unhide option on the Format button's drop-down menu (located in the Cells group of the Home tab). Suppose that you need to hide column B in the worksheet because it contains some irrelevant or sensitive information that you don't want printed. To hide this column, you could follow these steps:

1. **Select any cell in column B to designate it as the column to hide.**

2. **Click the drop-down button attached to the Format button in the Cells group on the Home tab.**

   Excel opens the Format button's drop-down menu.

3. **Click Hide & Unhide⇨Hide Columns on the drop-down menu.**

That's all there is to it — column B goes *poof!* All the information in the column disappears from the worksheet. When you hide column B, notice that the row of column letters in the frame now reads A, C, D, E, F, and so forth.

You could just as well have hidden column B by right-clicking its column letter on the frame and then choosing the Hide command on the column's shortcut menu.

Now, suppose that you've printed the worksheet and need to make a change to one of the entries in column B. To unhide the column, follow these steps:

1. **Position the mouse pointer on column letter A in the frame and drag the pointer right to select both columns A and C.**

   You must drag from A to C to include hidden column B as part of the column selection — don't click while holding down the Ctrl key or you won't get B.

2. **Click the drop-down button attached to the Format button in the Cells group on the Home tab.**

3. **Click Hide & Unhide⇨Unhide Columns on the drop-down menu.**

Excel brings back the hidden B column, and all three columns (A, B, and C) are selected. You can then click the mouse pointer on any cell in the worksheet to deselect the columns.

You could also unhide column B by selecting columns A through C, right-clicking either one of them, and then choosing the Unhide command on the column shortcut menu.

Hiding worksheet rows

The procedure for hiding and unhiding rows of the worksheet is essentially the same as for hiding and unhiding columns. The only difference is that after selecting the rows to hide, you click Hide & Unhide⇨Hide Rows on the Format button's drop-down menu and Hide & Unhide⇨Unhide Rows to bring them back.

Don't forget that you can use the Hide and Unhide options on the rows' shortcut menu to make selected rows disappear and then reappear in the worksheet.

Futzing with the Fonts

When you start a new worksheet, Excel 2013 assigns a uniform font and type size to all the cell entries you make. The default font is Microsoft's Calibri font (the so-called Body Font) in 11-point size. Although this font may be fine for normal entries, you may want to use something with a little more zing for titles and headings in the worksheet.

If you don't especially care for Calibri as the standard font, modify it from the General tab of the Excel Options dialog box (choose File⇨Options or press Alt+FT). Look for the Use This as the Default Font drop-down list box (containing Body Font as the default choice) in the When Creating New Workbooks section and then select the name of new font you want to make standard from this drop-down list. If you want a different type size, choose the Font Size drop-down list box and a new point size on its drop-down menu or enter the new point size for the standard font directly into the Font Size text box.

Using the buttons in the Font group on the Home tab, you can make most font changes (including selecting a new font style or new font size) without having to resort to changing the settings on the Font tab in the Format Cells dialog box (Ctrl+1):

✔ To select a new font for a cell selection, click the drop-down button next to the Font combo box and then select the name of the font you want to use from the list box. Excel displays the name of each font that appears in this list box in the actual font named (so that the font name becomes an example of what the font looks like — onscreen anyway).

✔ To change the font size, click the drop-down button next to the Font Size combo box, select the new font size or click the Font Size text box, type the new size, and then press Enter.

You can also add the attributes of **bold**, *italic*, underlining, or `strikethrough` to the font you use. The Font group of the Home tab contains the Bold, Italic, and Underline buttons, which not only add these attributes to a cell selection but remove them as well. After you click any of these attribute tools, notice that the tool becomes shaded whenever you position the cell cursor in the cell or cells that contain that attribute. When you click a selected format button to remove an attribute, Excel no longer shades the attribute button when you select the cell.

Although you'll probably make most font changes with the Home tab on the Ribbon, on rare occasions you may find it more convenient to make these changes from the Font tab in the Format Cells dialog box (Ctrl+1).

The Font tab in the Format Cells dialog box brings together under one roof fonts, font styles (bold and italics), effects (strikethrough, superscript, and subscript), and color changes. When you want to make many font-related changes to a cell selection, working in the Font tab may be your best bet. One of the nice things about using this tab is that it contains a Preview box that shows you how your font changes appear (onscreen at least).

To change the color of the entries in a cell selection, click the Font Color button's drop-down menu in the Font group on the Home tab and then select the color you want the text to appear in the drop-down palette. You can use Live Preview to see what the entries in the cell selection look like in a particular font color by moving the mouse pointer over the color swatches in the palette before you select one by clicking it (assuming, of course, that the palette doesn't cover the cells).

If you change font colors and then print the worksheet with a black-and-white printer, Excel renders the colors as shades of gray. The Automatic option at the top of the Font Color button's drop-down menu picks up the color assigned in Windows as the window text color. This color is black unless you change it in your display properties.

Altering the Alignment

The horizontal alignment assigned to cell entries when you first make them is simply a function of the type of entry it is: All text entries are left-aligned, and all values are right-aligned with the borders of their cells. However, you can alter this standard arrangement anytime it suits you.

The Alignment group of the Home tab contains three normal horizontal alignment tools: the Align Left, Center, and Align Right buttons. These buttons align the current cell selection exactly as you expect them to. On the right side of the Alignment group, you usually find the special alignment button called Merge & Center.

Despite its rather strange name, you'll want to get to know this button. You can use it to center a worksheet title across the entire width of a table in seconds (or faster, depending upon your machine). Figure 3-12 shows you how this works. To center the title, Mother Goose Enterprises – 2013 Sales, entered in cell A1 over the entire table (which extends from column A through E), select the cell range A1:E1 (the width of the table) and then click the Merge & Center button in the Alignment group on the Ribbon's Home tab.

In Figure 3-12, you see the result: The cells in row 1 of columns A through E are merged into one cell, and now the title is properly centered in this "super" cell and consequently over the entire table.

If you ever need to split up a supercell that you've merged with Merge & Center back into its original, individual cells, select the cell and then simply click the Merge & Center button in the Alignment group on the Home tab again.

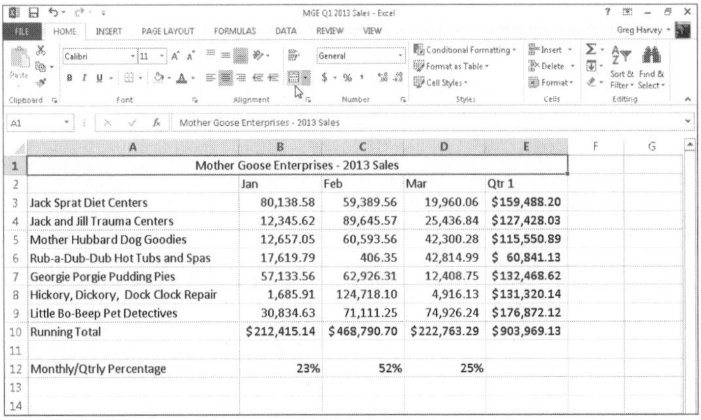

	A	B	C	D	E
1	Mother Goose Enterprises - 2013 Sales				
2		Jan	Feb	Mar	Qtr 1
3	Jack Sprat Diet Centers	80,138.58	59,389.56	19,960.06	$159,488.20
4	Jack and Jill Trauma Centers	12,345.62	89,645.57	25,436.84	$127,428.03
5	Mother Hubbard Dog Goodies	12,657.05	60,593.56	42,300.28	$115,550.89
6	Rub-a-Dub-Dub Hot Tubs and Spas	17,619.79	406.35	42,814.99	$ 60,841.13
7	Georgie Porgie Pudding Pies	57,133.56	62,926.31	12,408.75	$132,468.62
8	Hickory, Dickory, Dock Clock Repair	1,685.91	124,718.10	4,916.13	$131,320.14
9	Little Bo-Beep Pet Detectives	30,834.63	71,111.25	74,926.24	$176,872.12
10	Running Total	$212,415.14	$468,790.70	$222,763.29	$903,969.13
11					
12	Monthly/Qtrly Percentage	23%	52%	25%	

Figure 3-12: A worksheet title after merging and centering it across columns A through E.

Intent on indents

In Excel 2013, you can indent the entries in a cell selection by clicking the Increase Indent button. The Increase Indent button in the Alignment group of the Home tab sports a picture of an arrow pushing the lines of text to the right. Each time you click this button, Excel indents the entries in the current cell selection to the right by three character widths of the standard font.

You can remove an indent by clicking the Decrease Indent button (to the immediate left of the Increase Indent button) on the Home tab with the picture of the arrow pushing the lines of text to the left. Additionally, you can change how many characters an entry indents with the Increase Indent button (or outdents with the Decrease Indent button). Open the Format Cells dialog box (Ctrl+1). Select the Alignment tab, and then alter the value in the Indent text box (by typing a new value in this text box or by dialing up a new value with its spinner buttons).

From top to bottom

Left, right, and *center* alignment all refer to the horizontal positioning of a text entry in relation to the left and right cell borders (that is, horizontally). You can also align entries in relation to the top and bottom borders of their cells (that is, vertically). Normally, all entries align vertically with the bottom of the cells (as though they were resting on the very bottom of the cell). You can also vertically center an entry in its cell or align it with the top of its cell.

To change the vertical alignment of a cell range that you've selected, click the appropriate button (Top Align, Middle Align, or Bottom Align) in the Alignment group on the Home tab.

Figure 3-13 shows the title for the 2013 Mother Goose Enterprises sales worksheet after centering it vertically in its cell by clicking the Middle Align button on the Home tab. (This text entry was previously centered across the cell range A1:E1; the height of row 1 is increased from the normal 15 points to 36 points.)

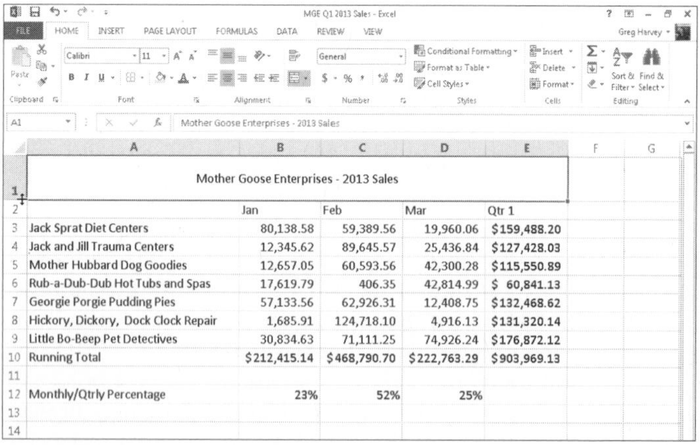

	A	B	C	D	E
1	Mother Goose Enterprises - 2013 Sales				
2		Jan	Feb	Mar	Qtr 1
3	Jack Sprat Diet Centers	80,138.58	59,389.56	19,960.06	$159,488.20
4	Jack and Jill Trauma Centers	12,345.62	89,645.57	25,436.84	$127,428.03
5	Mother Hubbard Dog Goodies	12,657.05	60,593.56	42,300.28	$115,550.89
6	Rub-a-Dub-Dub Hot Tubs and Spas	17,619.79	406.35	42,814.99	$ 60,841.13
7	Georgie Porgie Pudding Pies	57,133.56	62,926.31	12,408.75	$132,468.62
8	Hickory, Dickory, Dock Clock Repair	1,685.91	124,718.10	4,916.13	$131,320.14
9	Little Bo-Beep Pet Detectives	30,834.63	71,111.25	74,926.24	$176,872.12
10	Running Total	$212,415.14	$468,790.70	$222,763.29	$903,969.13
11					
12	Monthly/Qtrly Percentage	23%	52%	25%	
13					
14					

Figure 3-13: The worksheet title after centering it vertically between the top and bottom edges of row 1.

Tampering with how the text wraps

Traditionally, column headings in worksheet tables have been a problem — you had to keep them really short or abbreviate them if you wanted to avoid widening all the columns more than the data warranted. You can avoid this problem in Excel by using the Wrap Text button in the Alignment group on the Home tab (the one to the immediate right of the Orientation button). In Figure 3-14, I show a new worksheet in which cells B2:H2 contain the names of various companies within the vast Mother Goose Enterprises conglomerate. Every company name that spills over to a column on the right that contains another name is truncated except for the Little Bo Peep Pet Detectives name in the last column in cell H2.

Figure 3-14: A new worksheet with truncated column headings in row 2.

Rather than widen columns B through H sufficiently to display the company names, I use the Wrap Text feature to avoid widening the columns as much as these long company names would otherwise require, as shown in Figure 3-15. To create the effect shown here, I select the cells with the column headings, B2:H2, and then click the Wrap Text button in the Alignment group on the Home tab.

Selecting Wrap Text breaks up the long text entries (that either spill over or cut off) in the selection into separate lines. To accommodate more than one line in a cell, the program automatically expands the row height so that the entire wrapped-text entry is visible.

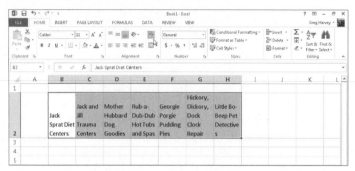

Figure 3-15: A worksheet after using Wrap Text to display all the headings without widening their columns.

When you select Wrap Text, Excel continues to use the horizontal and vertical alignment you specify for the cell. You can use any of the Horizontal alignment options found on the Alignment tab of the Format Cells dialog box (Ctrl+1), including Left (Indent), Center, Right (Indent), Justify, or Center Across Selection. However, you can't use the Fill option or Distributed (Indent) option. Select the Fill option on the Horizontal drop-down list box only when you want Excel to repeat the entry across the entire width of the cell.

If you want to wrap a text entry in its cell and have Excel justify the text with both the left and right borders of the cell, select the Justify option from the Horizontal drop-down list box in the Alignment tab in the Format Cells dialog box.

You can break a long text entry into separate lines by positioning the insertion point in the cell entry (or on the Formula bar) at the place where you want the new line to start and pressing Alt+Enter. Excel expands the row containing the cell (and the Formula bar above) when it starts a new line. When you press Enter to complete the entry or edit, Excel automatically wraps the text in the cell, according to the cell's column width and the position of the line break.

Reorienting cell entries

Instead of wrapping text entries in cells, you may find it more beneficial to change the orientation of the text by rotating the text up (in a counterclockwise direction) or down (in a clockwise direction). Peruse Figure 3-16 for a situation where changing the orientation of the wrapped column headings works much better than just wrapping them in their normal orientation in the cells.

Figure 3-16: Column headings rotated 90° counterclockwise.

This example shows the same column headings for the sample order form I introduced in Figure 3-15 after rotating them 90 degrees counterclockwise. To make this switch with the cell range B2:H2 selected, click the Orientation button in the Alignment group on the Home tab and then click the Rotate Text Up option on the drop-down menu.

Figure 3-17 shows the same headings rotated up at a 45-degree angle. To create what you see in this figure, you click the Angle Counterclockwise option on the Orientation button's drop-down menu after making the same cell selection, B2:H2.

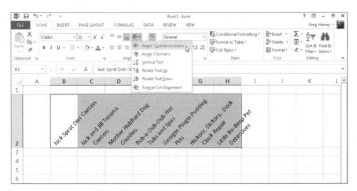

Figure 3-17: Column headings rotated 45° counterclockwise.

If you need to set the rotation of the entries in a spreadsheet at angles other than 45 and 90 degrees (up or down), you need to click the Format Cell Alignment option on the Orientation button's drop-down menu. Doing so opens the Alignment tab of the Format Cells dialog box (or press Ctrl+1 and click the Alignment tab) where you can then use the controls in the Orientation section to set the angle and number of degrees.

To set a new angle, enter the number of degrees in the Degrees text box, click the appropriate place on the semicircular diagram, or drag the line extending from the word *Text* in the diagram to the desired angle.

To angle text up using the Degrees text box, enter a positive number between 1 and 45 in the text box. To angle the text down, enter a negative number between –1 and –45.

To set the text vertically so that each letter is above the other in a single column, click the Vertical Text option on the Orientation button's drop-down menu on the Home tab.

Shrink to fit

For those times when you need to prevent Excel from widening the column to fit its cell entries (as might be the case when you need to display an entire table of data on a single screen or printed page), use the Shrink to Fit text control.

Click the Alignment tab of the Format Cells dialog box (Ctrl+1) and then click the Shrink to Fit check box in the Text Control section. Excel reduces the font size of the entries to the selected cells so that they don't require changing the current column width. Just be aware when using this Text Control option that, depending on the length of the entries and width of the column, you can end up with some text entries so small that they're completely illegible!

Bring on the borders!

The gridlines you normally see in the worksheet to separate the columns and rows are just guidelines to help you keep your place as you build your spreadsheet. You can choose to print them with your data or not (by checking or clearing the

Print check box that appears in the Gridlines section of the Sheet Options group on the Ribbon's Page Layout tab).

To emphasize sections of the worksheet or parts of a particular table, you can add borderlines or shading to certain cells. Don't confuse the *borderlines* that you add to accent a particular cell selection with the *gridlines* used to define cell borders in the worksheet — borders that you add print regardless of whether you print the worksheet gridlines.

To see the borders that you add to the cells in a worksheet, remove the gridlines normally displayed in the worksheet by clearing the View check box in the Gridlines section of the Sheet Options group on the Ribbon's Page Layout tab.

To add borders to a cell selection, click the drop-down button attached to the Borders button in the Font group on the Home tab. This displays a drop-down menu with all the border options you can apply to the cell selection (see Figure 3-18) where you click the type of line you want to apply to all its cells.

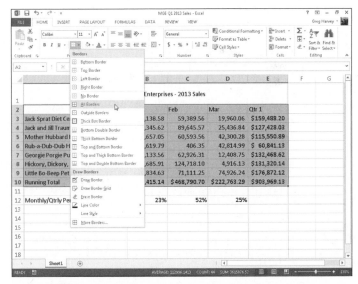

Figure 3-18: Select borders for a cell selection on the Borders drop-down menu opened with the Borders button on the Home tab.

When selecting options on this drop-down menu to determine where you want the borderlines drawn, keep these things in mind:

✔ To have Excel draw borders only around the outside edges of the entire cell selection (in other words, following the path of the expanded cell cursor), click the Outside Borders or the Thick Box Border options on this menu. To draw the outside borders yourself around an unselected cell range in the active worksheet, click the Draw Border option, drag the mouse (using the Pencil mouse pointer) through the range of cells, and then click the Borders button on the Home tab's Font group.

✔ If you want borderlines to appear around all four edges of each cell in the cell selection (like a paned window), select the All Borders option on this drop-down menu. If you want to draw the inside and outside borders yourself around an unselected cell range in the active worksheet, click the Draw Border Grid option, drag the mouse (using the Pencil mouse pointer) through the range of cells, and then click the Borders button on the Home tab.

To change the type of line, line thickness, or color of the borders you apply to a cell selection, you must open the Format Cells dialog box and use the options on its Border tab (click More Borders at the bottom of the Borders button's drop-down menu or press Ctrl+1 and then click the Border tab).

To select a new line thickness or line style for a border you're applying, click its example in the Style section. To change the color of the border you want to apply, click the color sample on the Color drop-down palette. After you select a new line style and/or color, apply the border to the cell selection by clicking the appropriate line in either the Presets or Border section of the Border tab before you click OK.

To get rid of existing borders in a worksheet, you must select the cell or cells that presently contain them and then click the No Border option at the top of the second section on the Borders button's drop-down menu.

Applying fill colors, patterns, and gradient effects to cells

You can also add emphasis to particular sections of the worksheet or one of its tables by changing the fill color of the cell selection and/or applying a pattern or gradient to it.

If you're using a black-and-white printer, you want to restrict your color choices to light gray in the color palette. Additionally, you want to restrict your use of pattern styles to the very open ones with few dots when enhancing a cell selection that contains any kind of entries (otherwise, the entries will be almost impossible to read when printed).

To choose a new fill color for the background of a cell selection, you can click the Fill Color button's drop-down menu in the Font group on the Home tab and then select the color you want to use in the drop-down palette. Remember that you can use Live Preview to see what the cell selection looks like in a particular fill color by moving the mouse pointer over the color swatches. Click one to select it.

To choose a new pattern for a cell selection, you must open the Format Cells dialog box (Ctrl+1), and then click the Fill tab. To change the pattern of the cell selection, click a pattern swatch from the Pattern Style button's pattern palette. To add a fill color to the pattern you select, click its color swatch in the Background Color section of the Fill tab.

If you want to add a gradient effect to the cell selection that goes from one color to another in a certain direction, click the Fill Effects button on the Fill tab to open the Fill Effects dialog box. This dialog box contains a Gradient tab with controls that enable you to determine the two colors to use as well as shading style and variant.

After you select the colors and styles of the gradient, check the Sample swatch in the Fill Effects dialog box. When you have it the way you want it, click OK to close the Fill Effects dialog box and return to the Format Cells dialog box. The selected gradient effect then appears in its Sample area on the Fill tab in the Format Cells dialog box. Unfortunately, this is one area where Live Preview doesn't work, so you're just going to have to click its OK button to apply the gradient to the cell selection to see how it actually looks in the worksheet.

Although you can't select new patterns or gradients (only colors) with the Fill Color button on the Home tab, you can remove fill colors, patterns, and gradients assigned to a cell selection by clicking the No Fill option on the Fill Color button's drop-down menu.

Doing It in Styles

In Excel 2013, vibrant cell styles are a snap to assign to your worksheet data using the Cell Styles gallery opened by selecting the Cell Styles button in the Styles group on the Ribbon's Home tab. The Cell Styles gallery contains loads of ready-made styles you can immediately apply to the current cell selection. Simply click the desired style sample in the gallery after using the Live Preview feature to determine which style looks best on your data.

Creating a new style for the gallery

To create a new style for the gallery by example, manually format a single cell with all the attributes you want (font, font size, font color, bold, italic, underlining, fill color, pattern, borders, orientation, and so on) and then click the Cell Styles button on the Home tab followed by the New Cell Style option at the bottom of the gallery. Excel then opens a Style dialog box where you replace the generic style name (Style 1, Style 2, and so on) with your own descriptive name before you click OK.

Excel then adds a sample of your new style — the style name formatted, with the new style's attributes — to a Custom section at the top of the Cell Styles gallery. To apply this custom style to a cell selection, you then only have to click its sample in the Custom section of the Cell Styles gallery.

The custom cell styles you create don't become part of the current workbook until the next time you save the workbook. Therefore, you need to remember to click the Save button on the Quick Access toolbar or press Ctrl+S to save your changes after creating a new cell style if you want that style to remain part of the workbook's Cell Styles gallery the next time you open the workbook in Excel.

Copying custom styles from one workbook into another

Excel makes it easy to copy custom cell styles that you've saved as part of one workbook into the workbook you're currently working on. To copy custom styles from one workbook to another, follow these steps:

1. **Open the workbook that needs the custom styles added to it from another existing workbook.**

   This can be a brand new workbook or one that you've opened for editing.

2. **Open the workbook that has the custom styles you want to copy saved as part of it.**

   See the previous section, "Creating a new style for the gallery" for tips on how to create and save cell styles.

3. **Switch back to the workbook into which you want to copy the saved custom styles.**

   You can do this by clicking the workbook's button on the Windows taskbar or using the Flip feature by pressing Alt+Tab until you select the workbook's thumbnail in the center of the display.

4. **Click the Cell Styles button on the Home tab followed by Merge Styles in the Cell Styles gallery or press Alt+HJM.**

   Excel opens the Merge Styles dialog box.

5. **Click the name of the open workbook file that contains the custom styles to copy in the Merge Styles From list box and then click OK.**

After you close the Merge Styles dialog box, Excel adds all the custom styles from the designated workbook into the current workbook, adding them to the Custom section of its Cell Styles gallery. To retain the custom styles you just imported, save the current workbook (click the Save button on the Quick Access toolbar or press Ctrl+S). Then, you can switch back to the workbook containing the original custom styles you just copied and close its file (press Alt+FC).

Fooling Around with the Format Painter

Using cell styles to format ranges of worksheet cells is certainly the way to go when you have to apply the same formatting repeatedly in the workbooks you create. However, there may be times when you simply want to reuse a particular cell format and apply it to particular groups of cells in a single workbook without ever bothering to open the Cell Styles gallery.

For those occasions when you feel the urge to format on the fly (so to speak), use the Format Painter button (the paintbrush icon) in the Clipboard group on the Home tab. This wonderful little tool enables you to take the formatting from a particular cell that you fancy up and apply its formatting to other cells in the worksheet simply by selecting those cells.

To use the Format Painter to copy a cell's formatting to other worksheet cells, just follow these easy steps:

1. **Format an example cell or cell range in your workbook, selecting whatever fonts, alignment, borders, patterns, and color you want it to have.**

2. **Select one of the cells you just fancied up, and click the Format Painter button in the Clipboard group on the Home tab.**

   The mouse or Touch Pointer changes from the standard thick, white cross to a thick, white cross with an animated paintbrush by its side, and you see a marquee around the selected cell with the formatting to be used by the Format Painter.

3. **Drag the white-cross-plus-animated-paintbrush pointer (the Format Painter pointer) through all the cells you want to format.**

   As soon as you release the mouse button, Excel applies all the formatting used in the example cell to all the cells you just selected!

To keep the Format Painter selected so that you can format a bunch of different cell ranges with the Format Painter pointer, double-click the Format Painter button on the Home tab after you select the sample cell with the desired formatting. To stop formatting cells with the Format Painter pointer, simply click the Format Painter button on the Home tab again (it remains selected when you double-click it) to restore the button to its unselected state and return the mouse pointer to its normal thick, white cross shape.

You can use the Format Painter to restore a cell range that you gussied all up back to its boring default (General) cell format. To do this, click an empty, previously unformatted cell in the worksheet before you click the Format Painter button and then use the Format Painter pointer to drag through the cells you want returned to the default General format.

Conditional Formatting

Before leaving behind the scintillating subject of cell formatting, there's one more formatting button in the Styles group of the Home tab of which you need to be aware. The Conditional Formatting button enables you to apply provisional formatting to a cell range based solely on the categories into which its current values fall. The cool thing about this kind of conditional formatting is that should you edit the numbers in the cell range so that their values fall into other categories, the program automatically changes their cell formatting to suit.

When you click the Conditional Formatting button in the Styles group of the Home tab, a drop-down menu appears with the following options:

✔ **Highlight Cells Rules** opens a continuation menu with various options for defining formatting rules that highlight the cells in the cell selection that contain certain values, text, or dates; that have values greater or less than a particular value; or that fall within a certain ranges of values.

✔ **Top/Bottom Rules** opens a continuation menu with various options for defining formatting rules that highlight the top and bottom values, percentages, and above and below average values in the cell selection.

✔ **Data Bars** opens a palette with different color data bars that you can apply to the cell selection to indicate their values relative to each other by clicking the data bar thumbnail.

✔ **Color Scales** opens a palette with different two- and three-colored scales that you can apply to the cell selection to indicate their values relative to each other by clicking the color scale thumbnail.

✔ **Icon Sets** opens a palette with different sets of icons that you can apply to the cell selection to indicate their values relative to each other by clicking the icon set.

✔ **New Rule** opens the New Formatting Rule dialog box where you define a custom conditional formatting rule to apply to the cell selection.

✔ **Clear Rules** opens a continuation menu where you can remove conditional formatting rules for the cell selection by clicking the Clear Rules from Selected Cells option, for the entire worksheet by clicking the Clear Rules from Entire Sheet option, or for just the current data table by clicking the Clear Rules from This Table option.

✔ **Manage Rules** opens the Conditional Formatting Rules Manager dialog box where you edit and delete particular rules as well as adjust their rule precedence by moving them up or down in the Rules list box.

Formatting with scales and markers

The easiest conditional formatting that you can apply to a worksheet cell range is using the pop-up palettes of graphical scales and markers attached to the Data Bars, Color Scales, and Icon Sets options on the Conditional Formatting button's drop-down menu:

✔ **Data Bars** represent the relative values in the cell selection by the length of the color bar in each cell and are great for helping you quickly spot the lower and higher values within a large range of data.

✔ **Color Scales** classify the relative values in a cell selection with a color gradation using a one-, two-, or three-color scale and are great for identifying the distribution of values across a large range of data.

✔ **Icon Sets** classify the values in the cell selection into three to five categories and each icon within the set represents a range of values that go from high to low. Icon sets are great for quickly identifying the different ranges of values in a range of data.

Figure 3-19 shows you an example of cell ranges (containing identical values) using each of the three formatting types. The values in the first range (B2:B12) are conditionally formatted using blue Gradient Fill Data Bars. The values in the second range (D2:D12) are conditionally formatted using the Green, Yellow, Red Color Scale. The values in the third range (F2:F12) are conditionally formatted using the 3 Arrows (Colored) Icon Set.

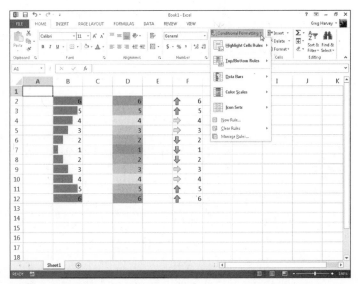

Figure 3-19: Sample worksheet with three identical cell ranges formatted with Excel's Data Bars, Color Scales, and Icon Sets options.

In Figure 3-19, the particular conditional formatting types Excel assigned to each cell range can be interpreted as follows:

- ✔ **Data bars** added to the cells in the first cell range, B2:B12, represent the relative size of its values graphically, much like a standard bar chart.

- ✔ **Color scale** applied to the second range, D2:D12, represent the relative size of the values in the range by color and hue (red hues applied to the lower values, yellow to the middle values, and green to the higher values).

- ✔ **Directional icons** applied to the third cell range, F2:F12, represent the relative size of the values in the range with arrow icons pointing in different directions (arrows pointing straight down for the lower values, straight up for the higher values, and sideways for middling values).

Highlighting cells ranges

The Highlight Cells Rules and Top/Bottom Rules options on Excel's Conditional Formatting drop-down menu enable you to quickly identify cell entries of particular interest in various cell ranges in your worksheet.

The options on the Highlight Cells Rules continuation menu enable you to set formats that identify values that are greater than, less than, equal to, or even between particular values that you set. This menu also contains an option for setting special formats for identifying cells that contain particular text (such as Yes, No, or even Maybe answers in a data list) or certain dates (such as project milestones and deadlines).

Perhaps one of the most useful options on the Highlight Cells Rules continuation menu is the Duplicate Values option that enables you to flag duplicate entries in a cell range by assigning them a special formatting. Doing this not only makes it easy to visually identify duplicate entries in a data list or table but also to find them electronically by searching for their particular formatting characteristics.

The options on the Top/Bottom Rules continuation menu enable you to specially format and, therefore, easily identify values in data tables and lists that are either above or below the norm. These options not only include those for automatically formatting all values in a range that are among the top 10 highest or lowest (either in value or percentage) but also above or below the average (as calculated by dividing the total by the number of values).

In addition to using the ready-made rules for conditional formatting located on the Highlight Cells Rules and Top/Bottom Rules continuation menus, you can also create your own custom rules. When you create a custom rule, you not only specify the rule type that identifies which values or text entries to format, but also you format the colors and other aspects included in the formatting.

Formatting via the Quick Analysis tool

One of the quickest and easiest ways to apply Data Bars, Color Scales, Icon Set, Greater Than, or Top 10% conditional formatting to a data table is with the new Quick Analysis tool. The coolest thing about applying conditional formatting in this manner is that Live Preview lets you visualize how your data looks with a particular type of conditional formatting before you actually apply it.

To assign conditional formatting with the Quick Analysis tool, select the data in your table that you wanted formatted and then select the Quick Analysis tool. By default, the Formatting option is selected when Excel displays the tool's palette so that all you have to do is highlight each of the formatting options with your mouse or Touch Pointer to see how they will look on your data.

Figure 3-20 shows you the Live Preview of the financial data in the Mother Goose 2013 Sales table with the Data Bars conditional formatting (as the Data Bars button is highlighted in the Formatting options). To assign this conditional format to the financial data in the selected table, you simply click the Data Bars button on the Quick Analysis palette. To preview how the data would look formatted with another conditional format, you simply highlight its button with the mouse or Touch Pointer.

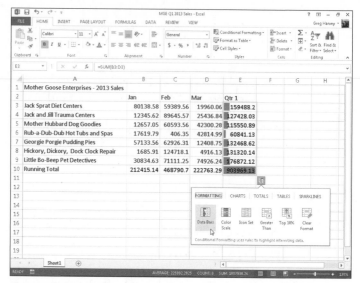

Figure 3-20: Previewing conditional formatting in a data table using the Quick Analysis tool.

Note that if you click the Greater Than button on the Quick Analysis palette, Excel displays a Greater Than dialog box where you specify the threshold value in the Format Cells That Are Greater Than text box, as well as select the color of the formatting for all the cells above that threshold in the drop-down list to its right.

With all the other kinds of conditional formats (Data Bars, Color Scale, Icon Set, and Top 10%), Excel just goes ahead and applies the first (default) option for that kind of formatting found on the Conditional Formatting button's drop-down menus on the Ribbon.

Chapter 4

Linking, Automating, and Sharing Spreadsheets

· ·

In This Chapter

▶ Using Office apps and Excel add-ins to automate and enhance Excel 2013

▶ Adding hyperlinks to other workbooks, worksheets, Office documents, web pages, or e-mail

▶ Creating and using macros to automate common spreadsheet tasks

▶ Sharing your worksheets on the web

▶ Editing your worksheets with Excel Web Applications

· ·

*A*t your first reading of the chapter title, you might have the impression that this is just a catch-all, potpourri chapter, containing the last bits of program information that don't fit anywhere else in the book. Actually, this is not the case because this chapter has a very definite theme, and that theme is how you go about extending the power of Excel.

It just so happens that Apps for Office, Excel add-ins, hyperlinks, and macros are four major ways to make Excel more vigorous and versatile: add-ins through the extra features they give Excel 2013; hyperlinks through links to other worksheets and Office documents; and web pages and macros through complex automated command sequences that you can play back whenever needed. And sharing your worksheets by attaching them to e-mail messages or publishing them to the web as well as being able to edit them anywhere in the world using the new online Excel Web Application are all part of the new collaboration features that enable you to both communicate and collaborate more quickly and effectively.

Using Apps for Office

Apps for Office are small programs that run inside various Microsoft Office 2013 programs to extend their functionality. There are apps to help you learn about Excel's features, look up words in the Merriam-Webster dictionary, and even enter dates into your spreadsheet by selecting them on a calendar.

Many of the Apps for Office are available free of charge, whereas others are offered for purchase from the Office Store for a small price. To use any of these apps in Excel 2013, you first need to install them:

1. **Click the Apps for Office button on the Insert tab of the Ribbon.**

    The Apps for Office drop-down menu appears with a Recently Used Apps section at the top and a See All link at the bottom. The first time you open this menu, the Recently Use Apps section will be blank.

2. **Click the See All link on the Apps for Office drop-down menu.**

    Excel opens the Apps for Office dialog box containing My Apps and Featured Apps links.

3. **Click the Featured Apps link to display a list of all the Editor's Picks and Recently Added apps available for Excel 2013.**

    Excel displays a list of all the Editor's Picks and Recently Added apps ready to install and use in Excel 2013 as shown in Figure 4-1. Each app in the list is identified by icon, name, its developer, its current user rating, and its price.

4. **To get more information about a particular app in the Editor's Picks or Recently Added list, click its name or icon in the Insert App dialog box. Otherwise, click the More Apps link to go online and see a complete list of apps.**

    If you click a particular app in the Editor's Picks or Recently Added list, your default web browser then opens a page on the Microsoft Office Store's website that gives you detailed information about the app you selected. If you clicked the More Apps link, your browser opens a page on the Office Store showing all the apps available for Excel 2013.

5. To install the app, click its Add button.

If you're not signed into your Microsoft account when you click Add, your browser takes you to a sign-in page where you enter your ID and password. When you are already signed into your Microsoft account and click Add to install a free app, your browser takes you directly to a confirmation web page. After you click Continue, you are taken to a page telling you how to insert the newly installed app into your Excel worksheet. For apps you must purchase, your browser takes you to a page where you provide your account information. After the purchase is approved, your web browser then takes you to the web page explaining how to insert your newly installed app into Excel.

6. Click the Close button on your web browser to close it and return to Excel.

Figure 4-1: Displaying the featured apps available for Excel 2013 in the Apps for Office dialog box.

Once installed, you can then insert the apps you want to use into the current worksheet. To do this, follow these steps:

1. If the Apps for Office dialog box is not currently open in Excel, open it by selecting Insert⇨Apps for Office⇨See All or press Alt+NSAS.

2. Click the My Apps link in App for Office dialog box.

Excel displays all the Apps for Office currently installed in Excel 2013.

3. **Click the app you want to use in your worksheet to select it and then click the Insert button or press Enter.**

Excel then inserts the app into your current worksheet so that you can start using its features. Some Office apps such as the Merriam-Webster Dictionary app and QuickHelp Starter open in task panes docked on the right side of the worksheet window. Others, such as Bing Maps and the Mini Calendar and Date Picker, open as graphic objects that float above the worksheet.

To close Office apps that open in docked task panes, you simply click the pane's Close button. To close Office apps that open as floating graphic objects, you need to select the graphic and then press the Delete key (don't worry — doing this only closes the app without uninstalling it).

Note that after you start using various apps in Excel, they're added to the Recently Used Apps section of the Apps for Office button's drop-down menu. You can then quickly re-open any closed app that appears on this menu simply by clicking it.

If you don't see any of your installed apps in the Apps for Office dialog box after clicking the My Apps link, click the Refresh link to refresh the list. Use the Manage My Apps link in this dialog box to keep tabs on all the apps you've installed for Office 2013 and SharePoint as well as uninstall any app that you're no longer using.

Using Excel Add-Ins

Excel add-in programs are small modules that extend the program's power by giving you access to a wide array of features and calculating functions not otherwise offered in the program. There are three types of add-ins:

- ✔ Built-in add-ins available when you install Excel 2013
- ✔ Add-ins that you can download for Excel 2013 from Microsoft's Office Online website (www.office.microsoft.com)
- ✔ Add-ins developed by third-party vendors for Excel 2013 that often must be purchased

When you first install Excel 2013, the built-in add-in programs included with Excel are fully loaded and ready to use. To load any other add-in programs, follow these steps:

1. **Choose File➪Options to open the Excel Options dialog box and then click the Add-Ins tab or press Alt+FTAA.**

   The Add-Ins tab lists the name, location, and type of add-ins you have access to.

2. **Click the Go button while Excel Add-Ins is selected in the Manage drop-down list box.**

   Excel opens the Add-Ins dialog box (similar to the one shown in Figure 4-2) showing all the names of the built-in add-in programs you can load.

Figure 4-2: Activate built-in add-ins in the Add-Ins dialog box.

3. **Select the check boxes for each add-in program that you want loaded in the Add-Ins Available list box.**

   Click the name of the add-in in the Add-Ins Available list box to display a brief description of its function at the bottom of this dialog box.

4. **Click the OK button to close the Add-Ins dialog box.**

   An alert dialog box may appear, asking whether you want to install each selected add-in.

5. **Click the OK button in each alert dialog box to install its add-in.**

Excel automatically places command buttons for the activated add-ins in either an Analysis group on the Ribbon's Data tab or in a Solutions group on the Formulas tab, depending on the type of add-in. For example, Excel places the command buttons for the Analysis ToolPak or Solver add-in in the Analysis group on the Data tab. For the Euro Currency Tools, Excel places its command buttons in the Solutions group on the Formulas tab.

If you end up never using a particular add-in you've loaded, you can unload it (and thereby free up some computer memory) by following the previously outlined procedure to open the Add-Ins dialog box and then clicking the name of the add-in to remove the check mark from its check box. Then click OK.

Adding Hyperlinks to a Worksheet

Hyperlinks automate Excel worksheets by making the opening of other Office documents and Excel workbooks and worksheets just a mouse click away. It doesn't matter whether these documents are located on your hard drive, a server on your LAN (Local Area Network), or web pages on the Internet or a company's intranet. You can also set up e-mail hyperlinks that automatically address messages to co-workers with whom you routinely correspond, and you can attach Excel workbooks or other types of Office files to these messages.

The hyperlinks that you add to your Excel worksheets can be of the following types:

- ✔ Text entries in cells (known as hypertext, normally formatted as underlined blue text)

- ✔ Clip art and imported graphics from files you've inserted into the worksheet

- ✔ Graphics you've created from the Shapes drop-down gallery on the Insert tab— in effect, turning the graphic images into buttons

When creating a text or graphic hyperlink, you can make a link to another Excel workbook or other type of Office file, a website address (using the URL address — you know, that monstrosity that begins with http://), a named location in the same workbook, or even a person's e-mail address. The named location can be a cell reference or named cell range in a particular worksheet.

To add the hyperlink to the text entry made in the current cell or a selected graphic object in your worksheet, follow these steps:

1. **Click the Hyperlink button on the Insert tab of the Ribbon or press Alt+NI, or simply press Ctrl+K.**

   Excel opens the Insert Hyperlink dialog box (similar to the one shown in Figure 4-3) in which you indicate the file, the web address (URL), or the named location in the workbook.

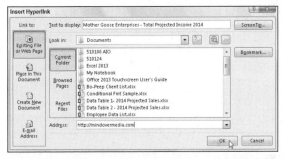

Figure 4-3: Linking to a web page in the Insert Hyperlink dialog box.

2a. **To have the hyperlink open another document, a web page on a company's intranet, or a website on the Internet, click the Existing File or Web Page button if it isn't already selected and then enter the file's directory path or web page's URL in the Address text box.**

   If the document you want to link to is located on your hard drive or a hard drive that is mapped on your computer, click the Look In drop-down button, select the folder, and then select the file in the list box. If you've recently opened the document you want to link to, you can click the Recent Files button and then select it from the list box.

   If the document you want to link to is located on a website and you know its web address (the www. dummies.com–like thing), you can type it into the

Address text box. If you recently browsed the web page you want to link to, you can click the Browsed Pages button and then select the address of the page from the list box.

2b. To have the hyperlink move the cell pointer to another cell or cell range in the same workbook, click the Place in This Document button. Next, type the address of the cell or cell range in the Type the Cell Reference text box or select the desired sheet name or range name from the Or Select a Place in This Document list box.

2c. To open a new e-mail message addressed to a particular recipient, click the E-mail Address button and then enter the recipient's e-mail address in the E-mail Address text box.

As soon as you begin typing the e-mail address in the E-mail Address text box, Excel inserts the text `mailto:` in front of whatever you've typed. (`mailto:` is the HTML tag that tells Excel to open your e-mail program when you click the hyperlink.)

If you want the hyperlink to add the subject of the e-mail message when it opens a new message in your e-mail program, enter this text in the Subject text box.

If the recipient's address is displayed in the Recently Used E-mail Addresses list box, you can enter it into the E-mail Address text box simply by clicking the address.

3. (Optional) To change the hyperlink text that appears in the cell of the worksheet (underlined and in blue) or add text if the cell is blank, type the desired label in the Text to Display text box.

4. (Optional) To add a ScreenTip to the hyperlink that appears when you position the mouse pointer over the hyperlink, click the ScreenTip button, type the text that you want to appear next to the mouse pointer in the ScreenTip box, and then click OK.

5. Click OK to close the Insert Hyperlink dialog box.

After you create a hyperlink in a worksheet, you can follow it to whatever destination you associated with the hyperlink. To follow a hyperlink, position the mouse pointer or Touch Pointer over the underlined blue text (if you assigned the hyperlink to text in a cell) or over the graphic image (if you assigned the hyperlink to a graphic inserted in the work-sheet). When the pointer changes to a hand with the index finger pointing upward, click the hypertext or graphic image, and Excel makes the jump to the designated external document, web page, cell within the workbook, or e-mail message.

After you follow a hypertext link to its destination, the color of its text changes from the traditional blue to a dark shade of purple (without affecting its underlining). This color change indicates that the hyperlink has been used. (Note, however, that graphic hyperlinks do not show any change in color after you follow them.) Additionally, Excel restores this underlined text to its original (unfollowed) blue color the next time that you open the workbook file.

If you need to edit a hyperlink attached to a worksheet cell or graphic object, you must be careful that, when getting Excel into Edit mode so that you can change the text, you don't inadvertently follow the link. When dealing with hypertext in a cell or assigned to a graphic object, you're best off right-clicking the cell or image and then clicking the appropriate editing command (Edit Hyperlink or Remove Hyperlink) on its shortcut menu.

Automating Commands with Macros

Macros automate the Excel worksheet by enabling you to record complex command sequences. By using macros that perform routine tasks, you not only speed up the procedure considerably (because Excel can play back your keystrokes and mouse actions much faster than you can perform them manually), but you are also assured that each step in the task is carried out the same way every time you perform the task.

Excel macro recorder records all the commands and key-strokes that you make in a language called Visual Basic for Applications (VBA), which is a special version of the BASIC programming language developed and refined by the good folks at Microsoft for use with all their Office application programs. You can then later learn how to use Excel's Visual Basic Editor to display and make changes to the macro's VBA code.

Recording new macros

Excel 2013 enables you to add an optional Developer tab to the Ribbon that contains its own Record Macro command button (among other command buttons that are very useful when doing more advanced work with macros). To add the Developer tab to the Excel 2013 Ribbon, follow these two steps:

1. **Choose File⇨Options or press Alt+FT to open the Excel Options dialog box.**

2. **Click the Customize Ribbon tab, select the Developer check box under Main Tabs in the Customize the Ribbon list box on the right side of the dialog box, and then click OK.**

Even if you don't add the Developer tab to the Ribbon, the Excel Status bar at the bottom of the Excel 2013 program window contains a Record Macro button (the button — it looks like a worksheet with a red dot — to the immediate right of the Ready status indicator). You click this button to turn on the macro recorder. Also, the View tab contains a Macros command button with a drop-down menu containing a Record Macro option.

When you turn on the macro recorder either by clicking the Record Macro button on the Status bar, clicking the Record Macro option on the Macros button's drop-down menu (Alt+WMR), or clicking the Record Macro button on the Developer tab (Alt+LR), the macro recorder records all your actions in the active worksheet or chart sheet when you make them.

The macro recorder doesn't record the keystrokes or mouse actions that you take to accomplish an action — only the VBA code required to perform the action itself. This means that mistakes that you make while taking an action that you rectify won't be recorded as part of the macro; for example, if you make a typing error and then edit it while the macro recorder is on, only the corrected entry shows up in the macro without the original mistakes and steps taken to remedy them.

The macros that you create with the macro recorder can be stored as part of the current workbook, in a new workbook, or in a special, globally available Personal Macro Workbook named PERSONAL.XLSB that's stored in a folder called XLSTART on your hard drive. When you record a macro as part of your Personal Macro Workbook, you can run that macro from any workbook that you have open. (This is because the PERSONAL. XLSB workbook is secretly opened whenever you launch Excel, and although it remains hidden, its macros are always available.) When you record macros as part of the current workbook or a new workbook, you can run those macros only when the workbook in which they were recorded is open in Excel.

When you create a macro with the macro recorder, you decide not only the workbook in which to store the macro but also what name and shortcut keystrokes to assign to the macro that you are creating. When assigning a name for your macro, use the same guidelines that you use when you assign a standard range name to a cell range in your worksheet. When assigning a shortcut keystroke to run the macro, you can assign

✔ The Ctrl key plus a letter from A to Z, as in Ctrl+Q

✔ Ctrl+Shift and a letter from A to Z, as in Ctrl+Shift+Q

You can't, however, assign the Ctrl key plus a punctuation or number key (such as Ctrl+1 or Ctrl+/) to your macro.

To see how easy it is to create a macro with the macro recorder, follow these steps for creating a macro that enters the company name in 4-point, bold type and centers the company name across rows A through E with the Merge and Center feature:

1. **Open the Excel workbook that contains the worksheet data or chart you want your macro to work with.**

   If you're building a macro that adds new data to a worksheet (as in this example), open a worksheet with plenty of blank cells in which to add the data. If you're building a macro that needs to be in a particular cell when its steps are played back, put the cell pointer in that cell.

2. **Click the Record Macro button on the Status bar.**

   The Record Macro dialog box opens, similar to the one shown in Figure 4-4, where you enter the macro name, define any keystroke shortcut, select the workbook in which to store the macro, and enter a description of the macro's function.

Figure 4-4: Defining the new macro to record in the Record Macro dialog box.

3. **Replace the Macro1 temporary macro name by entering your name for the macro in the Macro Name text box.**

   Remember that when naming a macro, you must not use spaces in the macro name and it must begin with a letter and not some number or punctuation symbol. For this example macro, you replace Macro1 in the Macro Name text box with the name Company_Name.

   Next, you can enter a letter between A and Z that acts like a shortcut key for running the macro when you press Ctrl followed by that letter key. Just remember that Excel has already assigned a number of Ctrl+letter keystroke shortcuts for doing common tasks, such as Ctrl+C for copying an item to the Clipboard and Ctrl+V for pasting an item from the Clipboard into the worksheet (see the Cheat Sheet online at www.dummies.com/cheatsheet/excel2013 for a complete list). If you assign the same keystrokes to the macro you're building, your macro's shortcut keys override and, therefore, disable Excel's ready-made shortcut keystrokes.

4. **(Optional) Click the Shortcut key text box and then enter the letter of the alphabet that you want to assign to the macro.**

   For this example macro, press Shift+C to assign Ctrl+Shift+C as the shortcut keystroke (so as not to disable the ready-made Ctrl+C shortcut).

   Next, you need to decide where to save the new macro that you're building. Select Personal Macro Workbook on the Store Macro In drop-down list box to be able to run the macro anytime you like. Select This Workbook (the default) when you need to run the macro only when the current workbook is open. Select New Workbook if you want to open a new workbook in which to record and save the new macro.

5. **Click the Personal Macro Workbook, New Workbook, or This Workbook option on the Store Macro In drop-down list to indicate where to store the new macro.**

For this example macro, select the Personal Macro Workbook so that you can use it to enter the company name in any Excel workbook that you create or edit.

Next, you should document the purpose and function of your macro in the Description list box. Although this step is purely optional, it is a good idea to get in the habit of recording this information every time you build a new macro so that you and your co-workers can always know what to expect from the macro when it's run.

6. **(Optional) Click the Description list box and then insert a brief description of the macro's purpose in front of the information indicating the date and who recorded the macro.**

Now you're ready to close the Record Macro dialog box and start recording your macro.

7. **Click OK to close the Record Macro dialog box.**

The Record Macro dialog box closes and the circular ·red Record Macro button on the Status bar and the Developer tab becomes a square, blue Stop Recording button.

On the Macro button's drop-down menu on the Ribbon's View tab and Code group on the Developer tab, you find a Use Relative References option. You click this drop-down menu item or command button when you want the macro recorder to record the macro relative to the position of the current cell. For this example macro, which enters the company name and formats it in the worksheet, you definitely need to click the Use Relative References button before you start recording commands. Otherwise, you can use the macro only to enter the company name starting in cell A1 of a worksheet.

8. (Optional) Click the Use Relative References option on the Macros button's drop-down menu on the View tab or click the Use Relative References button on the Developer tab if you want to be able to play back the macro anywhere in the worksheet.

9. Select the cells, enter the data, and choose the Excel commands required to perform the tasks that you want recorded just as you normally would in creating or editing the current worksheet, using the keyboard, the mouse, or a combination of the two.

   For the example macro, type the company name and click the Enter button on the Formula bar to complete the entry in the current cell. Next, click the Bold button and then click 12 on the Font Size drop-down list in the Font group on the Home tab. Finally, drag through cells A1:E1 to select this range and then click the Merge and Center command button, again on the Home tab.

   After you finish taking all the actions in Excel that you want recorded, you're ready to shut off the macro recorder.

10. Click the Stop Recording button on the Status bar or Developer tab on the Ribbon.

   The square, blue Stop Recording buttons on the Status bar and the Developer tab change back into circular red Record Macro buttons, letting you know that the macro recorder is now turned off and no further actions will be recorded.

Running macros

After you record a macro, you can run it by clicking the View Macros option on the Macros button's drop-down menu on the View tab, the Macros button on the Developer tab of the Ribbon, or by pressing Alt+F8 to open the Macro dialog box (see Figure 4-5). As this figure shows, Excel lists the names of all the macros in the current workbook and in your Personal Macro Workbook (provided you've created one) in the Macro Name list box. Simply click the name of the macro that you want to run and then click the Run button or press Enter to play back all its commands.

Figure 4-5: Select a macro to play back in the Macro dialog box.

If you assigned a shortcut keystroke to the macro, you don't have to bother opening the Macro dialog box to run the macro: Simply press Ctrl plus the letter key or Ctrl+Shift plus the letter key that you assigned and Excel immediately plays back all the commands that you recorded.

The reason that macros you record in the Personal Macro Workbook are always available in any Excel workbook is because the PERSONAL.XLSB workbook is also open — you just don't know it because Excel hides this workbook immediately after opening it each time you launch the program. As a result, if you try to edit or delete a macro in the Macro dialog box saved in the Personal Macro Workbook, Excel displays an alert dialog box telling you that you can't edit a hidden workbook.

To unhide the Personal Macro Workbook, first clear the alert dialog box and close the Macro dialog box; then click the Unhide button on the View tab (Alt+WU) and click the OK button in the Unhide dialog box while PERSONAL.XLSB is selected. Excel then makes the Personal Macro Workbook active, and you can open the Macro dialog box and edit or delete any macros you've saved in it. After you finish, close the Macro dialog box and then click the Hide button on the View tab (or press Alt+WH) to hide the Personal Macro Workbook once more.

Assigning macros to the Ribbon and the Quick Access toolbar

If you prefer, instead of running a macro by selecting it in the Macro dialog box or by pressing shortcut keys you assign to it, you can assign it to a custom tab on the Ribbon or a custom button on the Quick Access toolbar and then run it by clicking that custom button.

To assign a macro to a custom group on a custom Ribbon tab, follow these steps:

1. **Choose File⇨Options and then click the Customize Ribbon tab in the Excel Options dialog box (or press Alt+FTC).**

   Excel displays the Customize Ribbon pane in the Excel Options dialog box.

2. **Click Macros in the Choose Commands From drop-down list box on the left.**

   Excel lists the names of all the macros created in the current workbook and saved in the PERSONAL.XLSB workbook in the Choose Commands From list box.

3. **Click the name of the custom group on the custom tab to which you want to add the macro in the Main Tabs list box on the right.**

   If you haven't already created a custom tab and group for the macro or need to create a new one, follow these steps:

   a. *Click the New Tab button at the bottom of the Main Tabs list.*

      Excel adds both a New Tab (Custom) and New Group (Custom) item to the Main Tabs list while at the same time selecting the New Group (Custom) item.

   b. *Click the New Tab (Custom) item you just added to the Main Tabs.*

   c. *Click the Rename button at the bottom of the Main Tabs list box and then type a display name for the new custom tab before you click OK.*

   d. *Click the New Group (Custom) item right below the custom tab you just renamed.*

   e. *Click the Rename button and then type a display name for the new custom group before you click OK.*

4. **In the Choose Commands From list box on the left, click the name of the macro you want to add to the custom group now selected in the Main Tabs list box on the right.**

5. **Click the Add button to add the selected macro to the selected custom group on your custom tab and then click the OK button to close the Excel Options dialog box.**

After you add a macro to the custom group of a custom tab, the name of the macro appears on a button sporting a generic icon (a programming diagram chart) on the custom tab of the Ribbon. Then, all you have to do to run the macro is click this command button.

To assign a macro to a custom button on the Quick Access toolbar, follow these steps:

1. **Click the Customize Quick Access Toolbar button at the end of the Quick Access toolbar and then click More Commands on its drop-down menu.**

   Excel opens the Excel Options dialog box with the Quick Access Toolbar tab selected.

2. **Click Macros in the Choose Commands From drop-down list box.**

   Excel lists the names of all the macros created in the current workbook and saved in the PERSONAL.XLSB workbook in the Choose Commands From list box.

3. **Click the name of the macro to add to a custom button on the Quick Access toolbar in the Choose Commands From list box and then click the Add button.**

4. **Click OK to close the Excel Options dialog box.**

After you close the Excel Options dialog box, a custom button sporting a generic macro icon (picturing a standard command flowchart) appears on the Quick Access toolbar. You can choose a different icon by clicking the Rename button below the Customize the Ribbon box. To see the name of the macro assigned to this custom macro button as a ScreenTip, position the mouse pointer over the button. To run the macro, click the button.

Sharing Your Worksheets

Excel 2013 makes it easy to share your spreadsheets with trusted clients and co-workers. You can use the options on the Share screen in Backstage view to e-mail worksheets or send them by Instant Message to others who have access to Excel on their computers. If you have Microsoft's Lync online meeting software installed on your device, you can present the worksheet to the other attendees as part of a Lync meeting.

And if you save your workbook files in the cloud on your Windows Live SkyDrive, you can easily share the worksheets by inviting co-workers and clients to open them in Excel on their own devices or, if they don't have Excel, in their web browser with the Excel Web App.

Additionally, you can review or edit the workbooks you save on your SkyDrive when you're away from your office and the computer to which you have access doesn't have a compatible version of Excel installed on it. You simply use that computer's Internet access to log on to the My Documents folder of your SkyDrive containing uploaded copies of your spreadsheets, and then use the Excel Web App (that runs on most modern web browsers) to open and then review and edit them.

Sharing workbooks via SkyDrive

To share Excel workbooks you've saved on your SkyDrive, follow these steps:

1. **Open the workbook file you want to share and then choose File⇨Share (Alt+FH).**

   Excel opens the Share screen with the Invite People option selected (similar to the one shown in Figure 4-6).

2. **Click the Type Names or E-mail Addresses text box and then begin typing the e-mail address of the first person with whom you want to share the workbook.**

   As you type, Excel matches the letters with the names and e-mail addresses entered in your Address Book. When it finds possible matches, they are displayed in a drop-down menu, and you can select the person's e-mail address by clicking his or her name in the list.

To find e-mail addresses in your Address list and add them to this text box, click the Search the Address Book for Contacts button (to the immediate left of the Can Edit drop-down list box) and then use the options in the Address Book: Global Address List dialog box. To share the workbook with multiple people, type a semicolon (;) after each e-mail address you add to this text box.

3. **(Optional) Click the Can Edit drop-down button and select Can View option on the menu to prevent the people you invite from making any changes to the workbook you're sharing.**

   By default, Excel 2013 allows the people with whom you share your workbooks to make editing changes to the workbook that are automatically saved on your SkyDrive. If you want to restrict your recipients to reviewing the data without being able to make changes, be sure to replace the Can Edit option with Can View before sharing the workbook.

4. **(Optional) Click the Include a Personal Message with the Invitation text box and type in any personal message that you want to incorporate as part of the e-mail with the generic invitation to share the file.**

   By default, Excel creates a generic invitation.

5. **(Optional) Select the Require User to Sign-in Before Accessing Document check box if you want the people with whom you share the workbook to have to log in to a Windows Live account before they can open the workbook.**

   Don't select this check box unless you're giving your log-in information to the recipient(s) of the e-mail invitation, and don't give this log-in information to anyone that you don't trust completely.

6. **Click the Share button.**

   As soon as you click the Share button, Excel e-mails the invitation to share the workbook to each of the recipients entered in the Type Names or E-mail Addresses text box. The program also adds their e-mail addresses and the editing status of each recipient (Can Edit or Can View) in the Shared With section at the bottom of the Share screen.

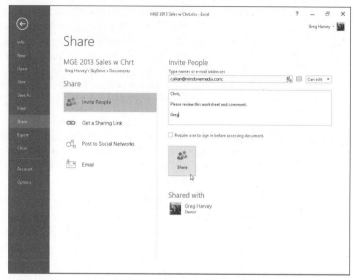

Figure 4-6: Invite co-workers or clients to share an Excel workbook saved on your SkyDrive.

All the people with whom you share a workbook receive an e-mail message containing a hyperlink to the workbook on your SkyDrive. When they follow this link, a copy of the workbook opens on a new page in their default web browser using the Excel Web App (if the web app is not compatible with the type of browser in use on their device, the browser opens it with the web viewer). If you've given the user permission to edit the file, the web app contains an Edit Workbook button.

When the user clicks this button in the Excel Web App, he has a choice between selecting an Edit in Excel and Edit in Excel Web App option on its drop-down menu. When he selects Edit in Excel, the workbook is downloaded and opened in his version of Excel. When he selects Edit in Excel Web App, the browser opens the workbook in a new version of the Excel Web App, containing a Home, Insert, and View tab with a limited set of command options that can be used in making any necessary changes (which are automatically saved to the workbook on the SkyDrive).

You must save your Excel workbook to your SkyDrive before you can share it via the Invite People option on the Share screen. If you haven't yet saved a copy of your workbook to the SkyDrive, when the Invite People option is selected on the

Share screen in the Backstage view, it contains a single Save to Cloud button. When you click this button, the backstage displays the Save As screen where you can save it to a folder on your SkyDrive. After Excel successfully saves the workbook in the cloud, Excel re-displays the Share screen with the Invite People option selected and all the invite options (shown in Figure 4-6) now available.

Getting a sharing link

Instead of sending e-mail invitations to individual recipients with links to the workbooks you want to share on your SkyDrive, you can create hyperlinks to them that you can then make available to all the people who need online editing or review access.

To create a link to a workbook open in Excel 2013 that's saved on your SkyDrive, select the Get a Sharing Link option on the Share screen in the Backstage view (Alt+FHL).

To create a view-only link that doesn't allow online editing, you then click the Create Link button to the right of the View Link option that appears on the right side of the Share screen under the Get a Sharing Link heading. To create an edit link that enables online editing instead of a view-only link or in addition to it, click the Create Link button to the right of the Edit Link option in its place.

Excel then displays the long and complex hyperlink for sharing your workbook under the View Link or Edit Link heading (depending upon which Create Link button you selected). The program also displays a list of any of the people with whom you've already shared the workbook using the Invite People option (as described in the previous section) under a Shared With heading and buttons indicating that anyone with a view link can view the workbook or with an edit link can edit it under a Shared Links heading.

After creating a view link or edit link for a workbook saved on your SkyDrive, you can select the entire hyperlink by simply clicking in the Get a Sharing Link section of the Share screen and then copying it to the Clipboard (Ctrl+C). After copying it to the clipboard, you can insert it into a new e-mail message (Ctrl+V) that you send to all the people with whom you want to share the Excel workbook to which it refers.

Posting links to social networks

In Excel 2013, you can now post a view link to any workbook saved on your SkyDrive whose data you want to share with your friends and followers on any of the social networks, such as Facebook, Twitter, or LinkedIn, to which you are a member.

To do this, open the workbook saved on your SkyDrive that you want to share. Then, select the Post to Social Networks option on the Share screen (Atl+FHN). Excel then displays the names preceded by check boxes for each of the social networks to which you are a member under the heading Post to Social Networks on the right side of the Share screen.

You then select the check box for each social network to which you want to post a link to your workbook on your page for your friends and followers. If you want to add a message about the worksheet you're sharing, you enter it below in the Include a Personal Message with the Invitation text box. Then, you click the Post button to post the link and any included message to your personal or company page in each of the selected social networks.

E-mailing workbooks

To e-mail a copy of a workbook you have open in Excel to a client or co-worker, choose File⇨Share⇨ Email (Alt+FDE). When you do this, a Send Using E-Mail panel appears with the following five options:

- ✔ **Send as Attachment** to create a new e-mail message using your default e-mail program with a copy of the workbook file as its attachment file.

- ✔ **Send a Link** to create a new e-mail message using your default e-mail program that contains a hyperlink to the workbook file. (This option is available only when the workbook file is saved on your company's or ISP's web server.)

- ✔ **Send as PDF** to convert the Excel workbook to the Adobe PDF (Portable Document File) format and make this new PDF the attachment file in a new e-mail message. (Your e-mail recipient must have a copy of the Adobe Reader installed on his or her computer in order to open the attachment.)

✔ **Send as XPS** to convert the Excel workbook to a Microsoft XPS (XML Paper Specification) file and make this new XPS file the attachment in a new e-mail message. (Your e-mail recipient must have an XPS Reader installed on his or her computer in order to open the attachment; this reader is installed automatically on computers running Windows 7 or Windows Vista.)

✔ **Send as Internet Fax** to send the workbook as a fax through an online fax service provider. You will need an account with a service provider as well as the Windows Fax and Scan Windows feature installed.

After selecting the e-mail option you want to use, Windows opens a new e-mail message in your e-mail program with a link to the workbook file or the file attached to it. To send the link or file, fill in the recipient's e-mail address in the To text box and any comments you want to make about the spreadsheet in the body of the message before you click the Send button.

Sharing workbooks with IM

If you have access to Skype IM (Instant Message) or have Microsoft's Lync software (see following section) installed on the device running Excel, you can share a workbook saved on your SkyDrive by sending a link to a co-worker or client via instant messaging.

To do this, simply open the workbook saved on your SkyDrive in Excel 2013 and then select the Send by Instant Message option on the Share screen in the Excel Backstage view (Alt+FHIM).

Then, fill in the recipient's name in the To: text box or select it from your Address Book using the Search the Address Book for Contacts button that immediately follows this box. Type any message about the spreadsheet you want to include into the Type Your Message Here text box and then select the Send IM button that appears near the bottom of the right-hand side of the Share screen under the heading Send by Instant Message.

If you want to send a copy of the workbook via instant message, it must be saved on a local drive on the device running Excel 2013 and your message software. To do this, use the Save As command to save a copy of the workbook on a local drive, then open that copy in Excel 2013 before you select the Send by Instant Message option on Excel's Share screen in the Backstage view.

Presenting worksheets online

If the device running Excel 2013 also has Microsoft's Lync 2013 online communication software installed, you can present your worksheets to the other attendees as part of any online meeting that you organize. To do this, first open the workbook you want to present at the online meeting in Excel 2013 before you select the Present Online option in the program's Share screen in the Backstage view (Alt+FHP). Click the Share button under the Present Online heading that appears on the right side of the Share screen.

If no meeting in Lync is currently running on your computer, a Share Workbook Window dialog box appears where you can launch one by simply clicking OK. Your name then appears in a floating Lync Conversation window.

To present your worksheet, highlight the Manage Presentable Content button (the fourth circle from the left on the bottom with the desktop monitor icon) and then click the name of your workbook file that appears in the Presentable Content section near the bottom of its pop-up palette. When you select the workbook file on this palette, the Conversation window closes and the active worksheet of the Excel workbook you're presenting appears in a presentation window with a golden outline around it. At the very top of the window containing your worksheet, you see a Currently Presenting mini-menu.

When you first present a worksheet, you have control over it. While you're in control, any menu selections or edits you make to its sheet are visible to all the other attendees of the online Lync meeting. If you wish to give editing control to another attendee, simply select his or her name from the Give Control drop-down menu.

You can then take back control of the worksheet by selecting the Take Back Control option at the very top of the Give Control drop-down menu. When you're finished presenting the worksheet and no longer want it to be visible to the other attendees, click the Stop Presenting button on the right side of the mini-menu at the top of the presentation window.

The Conversation window with your name in it then reappears and you can exit the meeting by clicking its Close button. You then return to the open workbook in Excel 2013 where you can save or abandon any editing changes made by you or by any other attendees to whom you ceded control during the time the worksheet was being presented.

Editing worksheets online

Microsoft offers several Office Web Apps for Word, Excel, PowerPoint, and OneNote as part of its Windows Live services that it provides along with your SkyDrive storage in the cloud. You can use the Excel Web App to edit worksheets saved on your SkyDrive online right within your web browser.

This comes in real handy for those occasions when you need to make last-minute edits to an Excel worksheet but don't have access to a device on which Excel is installed. As long as the device has an Internet connection and runs a web browser that supports the Excel Web App (such as Internet Explorer on a Surface tablet or even Safari on a MacBook Air), you can make eleventh-hour edits to the data, formulas, and even charts that are automatically saved in the workbook file on your SkyDrive.

The great part about using the Excel Web App to edit a copy of your online workbook is that the Excel Web App runs successfully under Microsoft's Internet Explorer 10 as well as under the latest versions of many other popular web browsers, including Mozilla Firefox for Windows, Mac, and Linux as well as Macintosh's Safari web browser on the iMac and iPad.

To edit a workbook saved on your SkyDrive with the Excel Web App, follow these simple steps:

1. **Launch the web browser on your device that supports the Excel Web App and then go to** www.live.com **and log in to your Windows Live account.**

   A web page showing information about your Windows Live account appears.

2. **Click the SkyDrive link at the top of the page or select SkyDrive from the Menu drop-down list.**

   Windows Live then opens the SkyDrive pages displaying all the folders you have there. Note that if you don't find a SkyDrive link at the top of the page in your browser, click the Menu drop-down button in the upper-left corner and then select SkyDrive on its drop-down menu.

3. **Click the link to the folder containing the workbook you want to edit to open it in on your SkyDrive web page.**

The folder you select displays all the files it contains.

4. **Select the check box in front of the name of the workbook file you want to edit with the Excel Web App to select the file.**

When you select the name of the Excel workbook file to edit, the SkyDrive page displays the current Share status of the file underneath a list of viewing and editing options in a column on the right side of the page (see Figure 4-7).

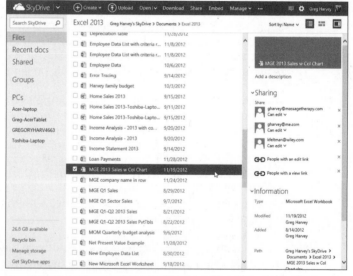

Figure 4-7: Selecting the Excel workbook to edit online with the Excel Web App in my Windows Live SkyDrive page.

5. **Click the Open button on the SkyDrive toolbar (or simply click the workbook's filename in the middle of the page).**

Your web browser opens the workbook in the Excel Web App on a new page (similar to the one shown in Figure 4-8) that replaces your SkyDrive page. This workbook contains all the worksheets that you've placed in the file with their tabs displayed.

You can then use the option buttons on the Home and Insert tab (most of which are identical to those found on the Home and Insert tab on the Excel 2013 Ribbon) to modify the layout or formatting of the data and charts on any of its sheets. You can also add new data to the worksheets as well as edit existing data just as you do in Excel 2013.

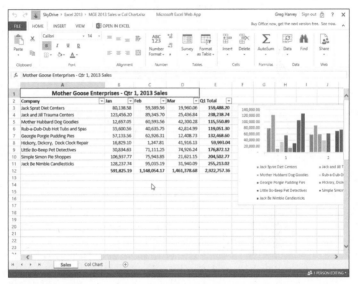

Figure 4-8: Editing my Excel workbook online in my web browser with the Excel Web App.

6. **When you're finished editing the workbook, click the web browser's Close button to save your changes. If you want to save a copy under a new filename in the same folder on the SkyDrive, choose File⇨Save As and then edit the filename that appears in the text box of the Save As dialog box before you click its Save button. (Or select the Overwrite Existing Files check box if you want to save the changes under the same filename).**

The Excel Web App is a whiz at making simple editing, formatting, and layout changes to your spreadsheet data and charts using common commands on its Home, Insert, and even Chart

Tools tab (when a chart is selected). However, the web app is completely incapable of dealing with any type of graphic objects like comments, shapes that you draw, and other types of graphics that you've added (charts are about the only type of Excel graphics that it can handle). To make modifications to these elements in your worksheet, you have two choices. Open the workbook in a local copy of Excel (assuming that the device you're using has Excel 2010 or 2013 installed on it) by clicking the Edit in Excel command on the Edit Workbook tab that appears at the top of the web app. Or, download a copy of the workbook to your local office computer (where you do have Excel 2013 installed) by choosing File⇨Save As⇨Download and make the more advanced edits to this downloaded copy of the file after you get back to the office.

Reviewing workbooks online

Sometimes you may find yourself working on a device that doesn't run a web browser that supports the Excel Web App. For example, when I use the Safari web browser on my iPhone 4 (unlike the version of Safari that runs on my MacBook Air laptop and iPad tablet), the browser opens my workbook files with the Excel Mobile Viewer instead of the Excel Web App.

The only problem with this is that the Mobile Viewer is just what it says it is — a viewer that only lets you see the data. If after reviewing the data, you find some things that need editing, you will have to make a note of them and get yourself to a device that runs a browser capable of running the Excel Web App or, better yet, one on which a full-blown version of Excel 2013 is installed.

Don't forget about Microsoft's SkyDrive app for the Apple iPad and iPhone, if you, like me, use these devices. The free SkyDrive app is available for download from the App Store on either device. The SkyDrive app enables you to access all the Excel workbook files you store on your SkyDrive on your iPad or iPhone. Just be aware that you can only review the worksheets that you open with this app because it is not yet capable, as of this writing, of running the Excel Web App. You can, however, use the app to send links to the workbook, change the permissions, rename the file, and open it in another app that can open Excel workbook files on these Apple mobile devices. Also, on the iPad, you can edit your SkyDrive workbooks with the Excel Web App on the Safari web browser.

Chapter 5

Printing the Masterpiece

· ·

· ·

*F*or most people, getting data down on paper is what spreadsheets are all about (all the talk about a so-called paperless office to the contrary). Everything — all the data entry, all the formatting, all the formula checking, all the things you do to get a spreadsheet ready — is really just preparation for printing its information.

In this chapter, you find out just how easy it is to print reports with Excel 2013. Thanks to the program's Print screen in Backstage view (Alt+FP), its Page Layout worksheet view, and its handy Page Layout tab on the Ribbon, you discover how to produce top-notch reports the first time you send the document to the printer (instead of the second or even the third time around).

The only trick to printing a worksheet is getting used to the paging scheme and learning how to control it. Many of the worksheets you create with Excel are not only longer than one printed page, but also wider. Word processors, such as Word 2013, page the document only vertically; they won't let you create a document wider than the page size you're using. Spreadsheet programs like Excel 2013, however, often have to break up pages both vertically and horizontally to print a worksheet document (a kind of tiling of the print job, if you will).

When breaking a worksheet into pages, Excel first pages the document vertically down the rows in the first columns of the print area (just like a word processor). After paging the first columns, the program pages down the rows of the second set of columns in the print area. Excel pages down and then over until the entire document included in the current print area (which can include the entire worksheet or just sections) is paged.

When paging the worksheet, Excel doesn't break up the information within a row or column. If not all the information in a row will fit at the bottom of the page, the program moves the entire row to the following page. If not all the information in a column will fit at the right edge of the page, the program moves the entire column to a new page. (Because Excel pages down and then over, the column may not appear on the next page of the report.)

You can deal with such paging problems in several ways, and in this chapter, you see all of them! After you have these page problems under control, printing is a proverbial piece of cake.

Previewing Pages in Page Layout View

Excel 2013's Page Layout view gives you instant access to the paging of the current worksheet. Activate this feature by clicking the Page Layout View button (the center one) to the immediate left of the Zoom slider on the Status bar or by clicking the Page Layout View command button on the Ribbon's View tab (Alt+WP). As you can see in Figure 5-1, when you switch to Page Layout view, Excel adds horizontal and vertical rulers to the column letter and row number headings. In the Worksheet area, this view shows the margins for each printed page, any headers and footers defined for the report, and the breaks between each page. (Often, you have to use the Zoom slider to reduce the screen magnification to display the page breaks onscreen.)

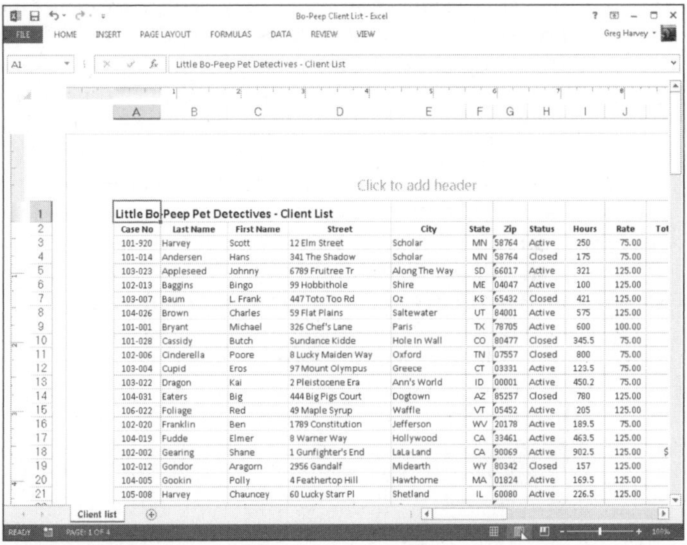

Case No	Last Name	First Name	Street	City	State	Zip	Status	Hours	Rate
101-920	Harvey	Scott	12 Elm Street	Scholar	MN	58764	Active	250	75.00
101-014	Andersen	Hans	341 The Shadow	Scholar	MN	58764	Closed	175	75.00
103-023	Appleseed	Johnny	6789 Fruitree Tr	Along The Way	SD	66017	Active	321	125.00
102-013	Baggins	Bingo	99 Hobbithole	Shire	ME	04047	Active	100	125.00
103-007	Baum	L. Frank	447 Toto Too Rd	Oz	KS	65432	Closed	421	125.00
104-026	Brown	Charles	59 Flat Plains	Saltewater	UT	84001	Active	575	125.00
101-001	Bryant	Michael	326 Chef's Lane	Paris	TX	78705	Active	600	100.00
101-028	Cassidy	Butch	Sundance Kidde	Hole In Wall	CO	80477	Closed	345.5	75.00
102-006	Cinderella	Poore	8 Lucky Maiden Way	Oxford	TN	07557	Closed	800	75.00
103-004	Cupid	Eros	97 Mount Olympus	Greece	CT	03331	Active	123.5	75.00
103-022	Dragon	Kai	2 Pleistocene Era	Ann's World	ID	00001	Active	450.2	75.00
104-031	Eaters	Big	444 Big Pigs Court	Dogtown	AZ	85257	Closed	780	125.00
106-022	Foliage	Red	49 Maple Syrup	Waffle	VT	05452	Active	205	125.00
102-020	Franklin	Ben	1789 Constitution	Jefferson	WV	20178	Active	189.5	75.00
104-019	Fudde	Elmer	8 Warner Way	Hollywood	CA	33461	Active	463.5	125.00
102-002	Gearing	Shane	1 Gunfighter's End	LaLa Land	CA	90069	Active	902.5	125.00
102-012	Gondor	Aragorn	2956 Gandalf	Midearth	WY	80342	Closed	157	125.00
104-005	Gookin	Polly	4 Feathertop Hill	Hawthorne	MA	01824	Active	169.5	125.00
105-008	Harvey	Chauncey	60 Lucky Starr Pl	Shetland	IL	60080	Active	226.5	125.00

Figure 5-1: Viewing a spreadsheet in Page Layout view.

To see all the pages in the active worksheet, drag the slider button in the Zoom slider on the Status bar to the left until you decrease the screen magnification sufficiently to display all the pages of data.

Excel displays rulers using the default units for your computer (inches on a U.S. computer and centimeters on a European machine). To change the units, open the Advanced tab of the Excel Options dialog box (File➪Options➪Advanced or Alt+FTA) and then select the appropriate unit (Inches, Centimeters, or Millimeters) on the Ruler Units drop-down menu in the Display section.

The Ruler check box on the View tab acts as a toggle switch so that the first time you click this button, Excel removes the rulers from the Page Layout view, and the second time you click this button, the program adds them again.

Using the Backstage Print Screen

To save paper and your sanity, print your worksheet directly from the Print screen in Excel's Backstage view by clicking File➪Print (or simply pressing Ctrl+P or Ctrl+F2). As you see in Figure 5-2, the Print screen shows you at-a-glance your current print settings along with a preview of the first page of the printout.

You can also add a Print Preview and Print command button to the Quick Access toolbar that opens this Print screen in the Backstage view. Simply click the Customize Quick Access Toolbar button followed by the Print Preview and Print option on its drop-down menu to add this button at the end of the toolbar. Then click this button anytime you want to preview a report before sending it to your printer.

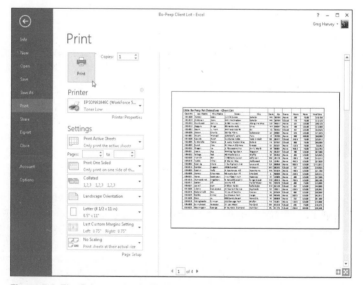

Figure 5-2: The Print screen in Backstage view shows your current print settings plus a preview of the printout.

You can use the Print Preview feature in the Print screen before you print any worksheet, section of worksheet, or entire workbook. Because of the peculiarities in paging worksheet data, you often need to check the page breaks for any report that requires more than one page. The print preview area in the Print panel shows you exactly how the worksheet data will page when printed. If necessary, you can return to the worksheet where you can make changes to the page settings from the Page Layout tab on the Ribbon before sending the report to the printer when everything looks okay.

When Excel displays a full page in the print preview area, you can barely read its contents. To increase the view to actual size to verify some of the data, click the Zoom to Page button in the lower-right corner of the Print panel. Check out the difference in Figure 5-3 — you can see what the first page of the four-page report looks like after I zoom in by clicking this Zoom to Page button.

Show Margins
Zoom to Page

Figure 5-3: Page 1 of a four-page report after clicking the Zoom to Page button.

After you enlarge a page to actual size, use the scroll bars to bring new parts of the page into view in the print preview area. To return to the full-page view, click the Zoom to Page button a second time to deselect it.

Excel indicates the number of pages in a report at the bottom of the print preview area. If your report has more than one page, you can view pages that follow by clicking the Next Page button to the right of the final page number. To review a page you've already seen, back up a page by clicking the Previous Page button to the left of the first page number. (The Previous Page button is gray if you're on the first page.)

To display markers indicating the current left, right, top and bottom margins along with the column widths, click the Show Margins button to the immediate left of the Zoom to Page button. You can then modify the column widths as well as the page margins by dragging the appropriate marker (see "Massaging the margins" later in this chapter for details).

When you finish previewing the report, the Print screen offers the following options for changing certain print settings before you send it to the printer:

- ✔ **Print** button with the **Number of Copies** combo box: Use this button to print the spreadsheet report using the current print settings listed on the panel. Use the combo box to indicate the number of copies you want when you need multiple copies printed.

- ✔ **Printer** drop-down button: Use this button to select a new printer or fax to send the spreadsheet report to when more than one device is installed. (Excel automatically displays the name of the printer that's installed as the default printer in Windows.)

- ✔ **Settings** drop-down buttons: These include a **Print What** drop-down button with attendant **Pages** combo boxes: Use the Print What drop-down button to choose between printing only the active (selected) worksheets in the workbook (the default), the entire workbook, the current cell selection in the current worksheet, and the currently selected table in the current worksheet. Use the Pages combo boxes to restrict what's printed to just the range of pages you enter in these boxes or select with their spinner buttons.

  Beneath the combo boxes, you find drop-down list buttons to print on both sides of each page in the report, collate the pages of the report, and switch the page orientation from Portrait (aligned with the short side) to Landscape (aligned with the long side). Additionally, you can select a paper size based on your printer's capabilities other than the default 8.5" x 11" letter, and customize the size of the report's margins (top, bottom, left, and right, as well as the margins for any header and footer on the page).

Printing the Current Worksheet

As long as you want to use Excel's default print settings to print all the cells in the current worksheet, printing in Excel 2013 is a breeze. Simply add the Quick Print button to the Quick Access toolbar (by clicking the Customize Quick Access Toolbar button followed by Quick Print on its drop-down menu).

After adding the Quick Print button to the Quick Access toolbar, you can use this button to print a single copy of all the information in the current worksheet, including any charts and graphics — but not including comments you add to cells.

When you click the Quick Print button, Excel routes the print job to the Windows print queue, which acts like a middleman and sends the job to the printer. While Excel sends the print job to the print queue, Excel displays a Printing dialog box to inform you of its progress (displaying such updates as *Printing Page 2 of 3*). After this dialog box disappears, you are free to go back to work in Excel. To stop the printing while the job is still being sent to the print queue, click the Cancel button in the Printing dialog box.

If you don't realize that you want to cancel the print job until after Excel finishes shipping it to the print queue (that is, while the Printing dialog box appears onscreen), you must do the following:

1. **Click the printer icon in the Notification area at the far right of the Windows taskbar (to the immediate left of the current time) with the secondary mouse button to open its shortcut menu.**

   This printer icon displays the ScreenTip *1 document(s) pending for so-and-so*. For example, when I'm printing, this message reads *1 document(s) pending for Greg* when I position the mouse pointer over the printer icon.

2. **Right-click the printer icon and then select the Open All Active Printers command from its shortcut menu.**

This opens the dialog box for the printer with the Excel print job in its queue (as described under the Document Name heading in the list box).

3. **Select the Excel print job that you want to cancel in the list box of your printer's dialog box.**

4. **Choose Document⇨Cancel from the menu and then click Yes to confirm you want to cancel the print job.**

5. **Wait for the print job to disappear from the queue in the printer's dialog box and then click the Close button to return to Excel.**

My Page Was Set Up!

About the only thing the slightest bit complex in print-ing a worksheet is figuring out how to get the pages right. Fortunately, the command buttons in the Page Setup group on the Ribbon's Page Layout tab give you a great deal of control over what goes on which page.

Three groups of buttons on the Page Layout tab help you get your page settings exactly as you want them. The Page Setup group, the Scale to Fit group, and the Sheet Options group are described in the following sections.

 To see the effect of changes you make in the Worksheet area, put the worksheet into Page Layout view by clicking the Page Layout button on the Status bar while you work with the command buttons in the Page Setup, Scale to Fit, and Sheet Options groups on the Page Layout tab of the Ribbon.

Using the buttons in the Page Setup group

The Page Setup group of the Page Layout tab contains the following important command buttons:

✔ **Margins** button to select one of three preset margins for the report or to set custom margins on the Margins tab of the Page Setup dialog box. (See "Massaging the margins" following this list.)

 ✔ **Orientation** button to switch between Portrait and
   Landscape mode for printing. (See the "Getting the lay of
   the landscape" section, later in this chapter.)

 ✔ **Size** button to select one of the preset paper sizes, set a
   custom size, or change the printing resolution or page
   number on the Page tab of the Page Setup dialog box.

 ✔ **Print Area** button to set and clear the print area.

 ✔ **Breaks** button to insert or remove page breaks. (See
   "Solving Page Break Problems" later in this chapter.)

 ✔ **Background** button to open the Sheet Background dialog
   box where you can select a new graphic image or photo
   to use as a background for the current worksheet. (This
   button changes to Delete Background as soon as you
   select a background image.)

 ✔ **Print Titles** button to open the Sheet tab of the Page
   Setup dialog box where you can define rows of the worksheet to repeat at the top and columns of the worksheet
   to repeat at the left as print titles for the report. (See
   "Putting out the print titles" later in this chapter.)

Massaging the margins

The Normal margin settings that Excel applies to a new report
use standard top, bottom, left, and right margins of ¾ inch
with just over a ¼ inch separating the header and footer from
the top and bottom margin, respectively.

In addition to the Normal margin settings, the program
enables you to select two other standard margins from the
Margins button's drop-down menu:

 ✔ **Wide** margins with 1-inch top, bottom, left, and right
   margins and ½ inch separating the header and footer
   from the top and bottom margin, respectively

 ✔ **Narrow** margins with a top and bottom margin of ¾ inch
   and a left and right margin of ¼ inch with 0.3 inch separating the header and footer from the top and bottom
   margin, respectively

Frequently, you find yourself with a report that takes up a full
printed page and then just enough to spill over onto a second,
mostly empty, page. To squeeze the last column or the last

few rows of the worksheet data onto Page 1, try selecting Narrow on the Margins button's drop-down menu.

If that doesn't do it, you can try manually adjusting the margins for the report from the Margins tab of the Page Setup dialog box or by dragging the margin markers in the preview area of the Print screen in the Backstage view (Press Ctrl+P and click the Show Margins button). To get more columns on a page, try reducing the left and right margins. To get more rows on a page, try reducing the top and bottom margins.

To open the Margins tab of the Page Setup dialog box (shown in Figure 5-4), click Custom Margins on the Margins button's drop-down menu. There, enter the new settings in the Top, Bottom, Left, and Right text boxes — or select the new margin settings with their respective spinner buttons.

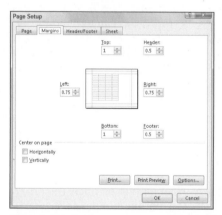

Figure 5-4: Adjust your report margins from the Margins tab in the Page Setup dialog box.

Select one or both Center on Page options in the Margins tab of the Page Setup dialog box (refer to Figure 5-4) to center a selection of data (that takes up less than a full page) between the current margin settings. In the Center on Page section, select the Horizontally check box to center the data between the left and right margins. Select the Vertically check box to center the data between the top and bottom margins.

When you click the Show Margins button in the Print screen in the Excel Backstage view (Ctrl+P) to modify the margin settings directly, you can also massage the column widths as well as the margins. (See Figure 5-5.) To change one of the margins, position the mouse pointer on the desired margin marker (the pointer shape changes to a double-headed arrow) and drag the marker with your mouse in the appropriate direction. When you release the mouse button, Excel redraws the page, using the new margin setting. You may gain or lose columns or rows, depending on what kind of adjustment you make. Changing the column widths is the same story: Drag the column marker to the left or right to decrease or increase the width of a particular column.

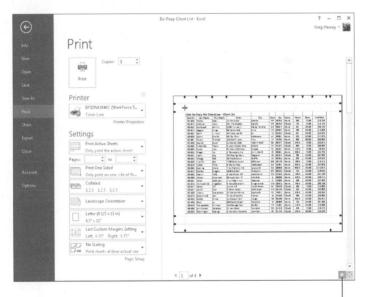

Show Margins

Figure 5-5: Drag a marker to adjust its margin in the page preview area of the Print screen when the Show Margins button is selected.

Getting the lay of the landscape

The drop-down menu attached to the Orientation button in the Page Setup group of the Ribbon's Page Layout tab contains two options:

- ✔ **Portrait** (the default) where the printing runs parallel to the short edge of the paper

- ✔ **Landscape** where the printing runs parallel to the long edge of the paper

Because many worksheets are far wider than they are tall
(such as budgets or sales tables that track expenditures over
12 months), you may find that wider worksheets page better if
you switch the orientation from Portrait mode (which accommodates fewer columns on a page because the printing runs
parallel to the short edge of the page) to Landscape mode.

In Figure 5-6, you can see the Print Preview window with the
first page of a report in Landscape mode in the Page Layout
view. For this report, Excel can fit three more columns of
information on this page in Landscape mode than it can in
Portrait mode. However, because this page orientation accommodates fewer rows, the total page count for this report
increases from two pages in Portrait mode to four pages in
Landscape mode.

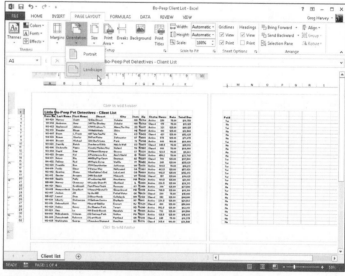

Figure 5-6: A Landscape mode report in Page Layout view.

Putting out the print titles

Excel's Print Titles feature enables you to print particular row
and column headings on each page of the report. Print titles
are important in multipage reports where the columns and

rows of related data spill over to other pages that no longer show the row and column headings on the first page.

Don't confuse print titles with the header of a report (see "From Header to Footer" later in this chapter). Even though both are printed on each page, header information prints in the top margin of the report; print titles always appear in the body of the report — at the top, in the case of rows used as print titles, and on the left, in the case of columns.

To designate rows and/or columns as the print titles for a report, follow these steps:

1. **Click the Print Titles button on the Page Layout tab on the Ribbon or press Alt+PI.**

   The Page Setup dialog box appears with the Sheet tab selected (see Figure 5-7).

   To designate worksheet rows as print titles, go to Step 2a. To designate worksheet columns as print titles, go to Step 2b.

2a. **Click in the Rows to Repeat at Top text box and then drag through the rows with information you want to appear at the top of each page in the worksheet below. If necessary, reduce the Page Setup dialog box to just the Rows to Repeat at Top text box by clicking the text box's Collapse/Expand button.**

   For the example shown in Figure 5-7, I clicked the Collapse/Expand button associated with the Rows to Repeat at Top text box and then dragged through rows 1 and 2 in column A of the Little Bo-Peep Pet Detectives – Client List worksheet. Excel entered the row range $1:$2 in the Rows to Repeat at Top text box.

   Excel indicates the print-title rows in the worksheet by placing a dotted line (that moves like a marquee) on the border between the titles and the information in the body of the report.

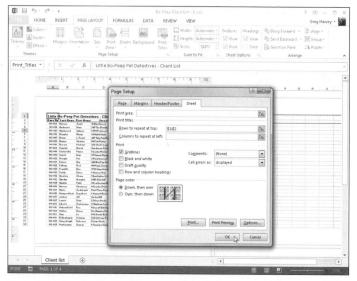

Figure 5-7: Specify the rows and columns to use as print titles on the Sheet tab of the Page Setup dialog box.

2b. Click in the Columns to Repeat at Left text box and then drag through the range of columns with the information you want to appear at the left edge of each page of the printed report in the worksheet below. If necessary, reduce the Page Setup dialog box to just the Columns to Repeat at Left text box by clicking the text box's Collapse/Expand button.

Excel indicates the print-title columns in the worksheet by placing a dotted line (that moves like a marquee) on the border between the titles and the information in the body of the report.

3. Click OK or press Enter to close the Page Setup dialog box.

The dotted line showing the border of the row and/or column titles disappears from the worksheet.

In Figure 5-7, rows 1 and 2 containing the worksheet title and column headings for the Little Bo-Peep Pet Detectives client database are designated as the print titles for the report in the Page Setup dialog box. In Figure 5-8, you can see the Print Preview window with the second page of the report. Note how these print titles appear on all pages of the report.

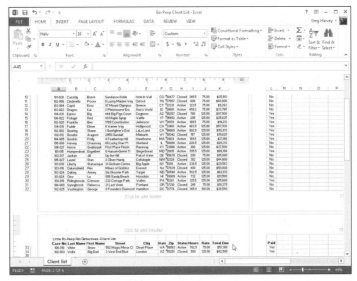

Figure 5-8: Page 2 of a sample report in Print Preview with defined print titles.

To clear print titles from a report if you no longer need them, open the Sheet tab of the Page Setup dialog box and then delete the row and column ranges from the Rows to Repeat at Top and the Columns to Repeat at Left text boxes. Click OK or press Enter.

Using the buttons in the Scale to Fit group

If your printer supports scaling options, you're in luck. You can always get a worksheet to fit on a single page simply by selecting the 1 Page option on the Width and Height drop-down menus attached to their command buttons in the Scale to Fit group on the Ribbon's Page Layout tab. When you select these options, Excel figures out how much to reduce the size of the information you're printing to fit it all on one page.

After clicking the Page Break Preview button on the Status bar, you might preview this page in the Print screen in the Backstage view (Ctrl+P) and find that the printing is just too small to read comfortably. Go back to the Normal worksheet view (Esc), select the Page Layout tab on the Ribbon, and try changing the number of pages in the Width and Height drop-down menus in the Scale to Fit group.

Instead of trying to stuff everything on one page, check out how your worksheet looks if you fit it on two pages across. Try this: Select 2 Pages on the Width button's drop-down menu on the Page Layout tab and leave 1 Page selected in the Height drop-down list button. Alternatively, see how the worksheet looks on two pages down: Select 1 Page on the Width button's drop-down menu and 2 Pages on the Height button's drop-down menu.

After using the Width and Height Scale to Fit options, you may find that you don't want to scale the printing. Cancel scaling by selecting Automatic on both the Width and Height drop-down menus and then entering **100** in the Scale text box (or select 100% with its spinner buttons).

Using the Print buttons in the Sheet Options group

The Sheet Options group contains two very useful Print check boxes (neither of which is selected automatically). The first is in the Gridlines column and the second is in the Headings column:

- ✔ Select the Print check box in the Gridlines column to print the column and row gridlines on each page of the report.

- ✔ Select the Print check box in the Headings column to print the row headings with the row numbers and the column headings with the column letters on each page of the report.

Select both check boxes (by clicking them to put check marks in them) when you want the printed version of your spreadsheet data to closely match its onscreen appearance. This is useful when you need to use the cell references on the printout to help you later locate the cells in the actual worksheet that need editing.

From Header to Footer

Headers and footers are simply standard text that appears on every page of the report. A header prints in the top margin of the page, and a footer prints — you guessed it — in the bottom margin. Both are centered vertically in the margins. Unless you specify otherwise, Excel does not automatically add either a header or footer to a new workbook.

Use headers and footers in a report to identify the document used to produce the report and display the page numbers and the date and time of printing.

The place to add a header or footer to a report is in Page Layout view. You can switch to this view by clicking the Page Layout View button on the Status bar or by clicking the Page Layout View button on the Ribbon's View tab, or by just pressing Alt+WP.

When the worksheet is in Page Layout view, position the mouse pointer over the section in the top margin of the first page marked Click to Add Header or in the bottom margin of the first page marked Click to Add Footer.

To create a centered header or footer, click the center section of this header/footer area to set the insertion point in the middle of the section. To add a left-aligned header or footer, click the left section to set the insertion point flush with the left edge. To add a right-aligned header or footer, click the right section to set the insertion point flush with the right edge.

Immediately after setting the insertion point in the left, center, or right section of the header/footer area, Excel adds a Header & Footer Tools contextual tab with its own Design tab (see Figure 5-9). The Design tab is divided into Header & Footer, Header & Footer Elements, Navigation, and Options groups.

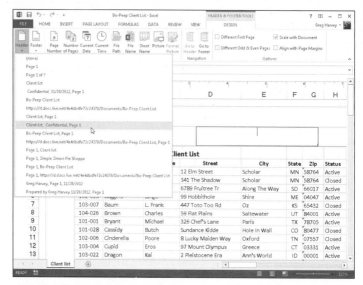

Figure 5-9: Defining a new header using the buttons on the Design tab of the Header & Footer Tools contextual tab.

Adding an Auto Header and Footer

The Header and Footer command buttons on the Design tab of the Header & Footer Tools contextual tab enable you to add stock headers and footers in an instant. Simply click the appropriate command button and then click the header or footer example you want to use on the Header or Footer drop-down menu that appears.

To create the centered header and footer for the report shown in Figure 5-10, I selected Client List, Confidential, Page 1 on the Header command button's drop-down menu. Client List is the name of the worksheet; Confidential is stock text; and Page 1 is, of course, the current page number.

To set up the footer, I chose Page 1 of ? in the Footer command button's drop-down menu (which puts the current page number with the total number of pages in the report). You can select this paging option on either the Header or Footer button's drop-down menu.

Check out the results in Figure 5-10, which is the first page of the report in Page Layout view. Here you can see the header and footer as they will print. You can also see how choosing Page 1 of ? works in the footer: On the first page, you see the centered footer Page 1 of 4; on the second page, the centered footer reads Page 2 of 4.

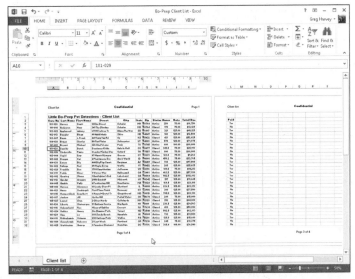

Figure 5-10: The first page of a report in Page Layout view shows you how the header and footer will print.

If, after selecting some stock header or footer info, you decide that you no longer need either the header or footer printed in your report, you can remove it. Simply click the (None) option at the top of the Header button's or Footer button's drop-down menu. (Remember that the Design tab with the Header and Footer command buttons under the Header & Footer Tools contextual tab is selected on the Ribbon the moment you click the header or footer in Page Layout view.)

Creating a custom header or footer

Most of the time, the stock headers and footers available on the Header button's and Footer button's drop-down menus are sufficient for your report-printing needs. Occasionally, however, you may want to insert information not available in these list boxes or in an arrangement that Excel doesn't offer in the ready-made headers and footers.

For those times, you need to use the command buttons that appear in the Header & Footer Elements group of the Design tab on the Header & Footer Tools contextual tab. These command buttons enable you to blend your own information with that generated by Excel into different sections of the custom header or footer you're creating.

The command buttons in the Header & Footer Elements group include

- ✔ **Page Number:** Click this button to insert the `&[Page]` code that puts in the current page number.

- ✔ **Number of Pages:** Click this button to insert the `&[Pages]` code that puts in the total number of pages.

- ✔ **Current Date:** Click this button to insert the `&[Date]` code that puts in the current date.

- ✔ **Current Time:** Click this button to insert the `&[Time]` code that puts in the current time.

- ✔ **File Path:** Click this button to insert the `&[Path]&[File]` codes that put in the directory path along with the name of the workbook file.

- ✔ **File Name:** Click this button to insert the `&[File]` code that puts in the name of the workbook file.

- ✔ **Sheet Name:** Click this button to insert the `&[Tab]` code that puts in the name of the worksheet as shown on the sheet tab.

- ✔ **Picture:** Click this button to insert the `&[Picture]` code that inserts the image that you select from the Insert Picture dialog box that shows the contents of the My Pictures folder on your computer by default.

- ✔ **Format Picture:** Click this button to apply the formatting that you choose from the Format Picture dialog box to the `&[Picture]` code that you enter with the Insert Picture button without adding any code of its own.

To use these command buttons in the Header & Footer Elements group to create a custom header or footer, follow these steps:

1. **Put your worksheet into Page Layout view by clicking the Page Layout View button on the Status bar or by clicking View⇨Page Layout View on the Ribbon or by pressing Alt+WP.**

   In Page Layout view, the text Click to Add Header appears centered in the top margin of the first page and the text Click to Add Footer appears centered in the bottom margin.

2. **Position the mouse pointer in the top margin to create a custom header or the bottom margin to create a custom footer and then click the pointer in the left, center, or right section of the header or footer to set the insertion point and left-align, center, or right-align the text.**

   When Excel sets the insertion point, the text Click to Add Header and Click to Add Footer disappears and the Design tab on the Header & Footer Tools contextual tab becomes active on the Ribbon.

3. **To add program-generated information to your custom header or footer (such as the filename, worksheet name, current date, and so forth), click the information's corresponding command button in the Header & Footer Elements group.**

   Excel inserts the appropriate header/footer code preceded by an ampersand (&) into the header or footer. These codes are replaced by the actual information (filename, worksheet name, graphic image, and the like) as soon as you click another section of the header or footer or finish the header or footer by clicking the mouse pointer outside of it.

4. **(Optional) To add your own text to the custom header or footer, type it at the insertion point.**

   When joining program-generated information indicated by a header/footer code with your own text, be sure to insert the appropriate spaces and punctuation. For example, to have Excel display Page 1 of 4 in a custom header or footer, do the following:

     a. Type the word **Page** *and press the spacebar.*

     b. Click the Page Number command button and press the spacebar again.

     c. Type the word **of** *and press the spacebar a third time.*

     d. Click the Number of Pages command button.

This inserts *Page &[Page] of &[Pages]* in the custom header (or footer).

5. **(Optional) To modify the font, font size, or some other font attribute of your custom header or footer, drag through its codes and text, click the Home tab, and then click the appropriate command button in the Font group.**

   In addition to selecting a new font and font size for the custom header or footer, you can add bold, italic, underlining, and a new font color to its text with the Bold, Italic, Underline, and Font Color command buttons on the Home tab.

6. **After you finish defining and formatting the codes and text for your custom header or footer, click a cell in the Worksheet area to deselect the header or footer area.**

   Excel replaces the header/footer codes in the custom header or footer with the actual information, while at the same time removing the Header & Footer Tools contextual tab from the Ribbon.

Figure 5-11 shows you a custom footer I added to a spreadsheet in Page Layout view. This custom footer blends my own text, Preliminary Client List, with a program-generated sheet name, date, and time information, and uses all three sections: left-aligned page information, centered Preliminary Client List text, and right-aligned current date and time.

Creating first-page headers and footers

Excel 2013 enables you to define a header or footer for the first page that's different from all the rest of the pages. Simply click the Different First Page check box to put a check mark in it. (This check box is part of the Options group of the Design tab on the Header & Footer Tools contextual tab that appears when you're defining or editing a header or footer in Page Layout view.)

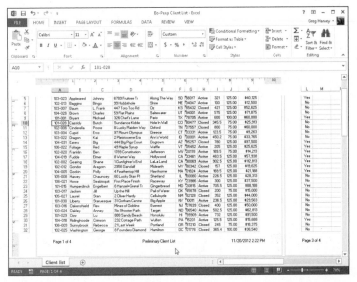

Figure 5-11: A spreadsheet in Page Layout view showing the custom footer.

After selecting the Different First Page check box, go ahead and define the unique header and/or footer for just the first page (now marked First Page Header or First Page Footer). Then, on the second page of the report, define the header and/or footer (marked simply Header or Footer) for the remaining pages of the report (see "Adding an Auto Header and Footer" and "Creating a custom header or footer" earlier in the chapter for details).

Use this feature when your spreadsheet report has a cover page that needs no header or footer. For example, suppose that you have a report that needs the current page number and total pages centered at the bottom of all pages except the cover page. To do this, select the Different First Page check box on the Design tab of the Header & Footer Tools contextual tab on the Ribbon. Then define a centered Auto Footer that displays the current page number and total pages (Page 1 of ?) on the second page of the report, leaving the Click to Add Footer text intact on the first page.

Excel will correctly number both the total number of pages in the report and the current page number without printing this information on the first page. For example, if your report has six pages (including the cover page), the second page footer will read Page 2 of 6; the third page, Page 3 of 6; and so on, even if the first printed page has no footer.

Creating even and odd page headers and footers

If you plan to do two-sided printing or copying of your spreadsheet report, you may want to define one header or footer for the even pages and another for the odd pages of the report. That way, the header or footer information (such as the report name or current page) alternates between being right-aligned on the odd pages (printed on the front side of the page) and being left-aligned on the even pages (printed on the back of the page).

To create an alternating header or footer for a report, click the Different Odd & Even Pages check box to put a check mark in it. (This check box is in the Options group of the Design tab on the Header & Footer Tools contextual tab that appears when you're defining or editing a header or footer in Page Layout view.)

After that, create a header or footer on the first page of the report (now marked Odd Page Header or Odd Page Footer) in the third, right-aligned section of the header or footer area and then re-create this header or footer on the second page (now marked Even Page Header or Even Page Footer), this time in the first, left-aligned section.

Solving Page Break Problems

The Page Break preview feature in Excel enables you to spot and fix page break problems in an instant, such as when the program wants to split information across different pages that you know should always be on the same page.

Figure 5-12 shows a worksheet in Page Break Preview with an example of a bad vertical page break that you can remedy by adjusting the location of the page break on Page 1 and Page 3. Given the page size, orientation, and margin settings for this report, Excel breaks the page between columns K and L. This break separates the Paid column (L) from all the others in the client list, effectively putting this information on its own Page 3 and Page 4 (not shown in Figure 5-12).

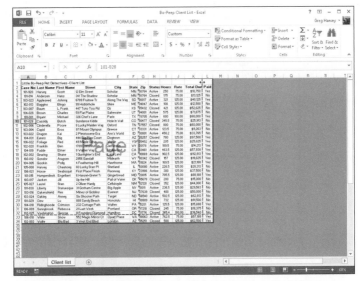

Figure 5-12: Preview page breaks in a report with Page Break Preview.

To prevent the data in the Paid column from printing on its own pages, you need to move the page break to a column on the left. In this case, I moved the page break between columns G (with the zip-code data) and H (containing the account status information) so that the name and address information stays together on Page 1 and Page 2 and the other client data is printed together on Page 3 and Page 4. Figure 5-13 shows vertical page breaks in the Page Break Preview worksheet view, which you can accomplish by following these steps:

1. **Click the Page Break Preview button (the third one in the cluster to the left of the Zoom slider) on the Status bar, or click View⇨Page Break Preview on the Ribbon or press Alt+WI.**

   This takes you into a Page Break Preview worksheet view that shows your worksheet data at a reduced magnification (60 percent of normal in Figure 5-13) with the page numbers displayed in large light type and the page breaks shown by heavy lines between the columns and rows of the worksheet.

   The first time you choose this command, Excel displays a Welcome to Page Break Preview dialog box. To prevent this dialog box from reappearing each time you use Page Break Preview, click the Do Not Show This Dialog Again check box before you close the Welcome to Page Break Preview alert dialog box.

2. **Click OK or press Enter to get rid of the Welcome to Page Break Preview alert dialog box.**

3. **Position the mouse pointer somewhere on the page break indicator (one of the heavy lines surrounding the representation of the page) that you need to adjust; when the pointer changes to a double-headed arrow, drag the page indicator to the desired column or row and release the mouse button.**

For the example shown in Figure 5-13, I dragged the page break indicator between Page 1 and Page 3 to the left so that it's between columns G and H. Excel placed the page break at this point, which puts all the name and address information together on Page 1 and Page 2. This new page break then causes all the other columns of client data to print together on Page 3 and Page 4.

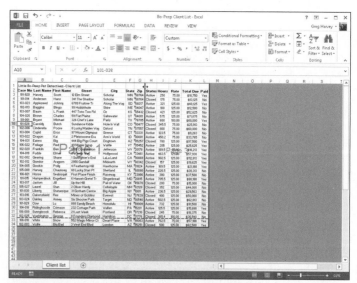

Figure 5-13: Page 1 of the report after adjusting the page breaks in the Page Break Preview worksheet view.

4. **After you finish adjusting the page breaks in Page Break Preview (and, presumably, printing the report), click the Normal button (the first one in the cluster to the left of the Zoom slider) on the Status bar, or click View⇨Normal on the Ribbon or press Alt+WL to return the worksheet to its regular view of the data.**

You can also insert your own manual page breaks at the cell cursor's position by clicking Insert Page Break on the Breaks button's drop-down menu on the Page Layout tab (Alt+PBI) and remove them by clicking Remove Page Break on this menu (Alt+PBR). To remove all manual page breaks that you've inserted into a report, click Reset All Page Breaks on the Breaks button's drop-down menu (Alt+PBA).

Letting Your Formulas All Hang Out

A basic printing technique that you may need occasionally is printing the formulas in a worksheet instead of printing the calculated results of the formulas. You can check over a print-out of the formulas in your worksheet to make sure that you haven't done anything stupid (like replace a formula with a number or use the wrong cell references in a formula) before you distribute the worksheet company-wide.

Before you can print a worksheet's formulas, you have to display the formulas, rather than their results, in the cells by clicking the Show Formulas button (the one with the icon that looks like a page of a calendar with a tiny 15 that's above the Error Checking button) in the Formula Auditing group on the Ribbon's Formulas tab (Alt+MH).

Excel then displays the contents of each cell in the worksheet the way it appears in the Formula bar or when you're editing it in the cell. Notice that value entries lose their number formatting, formulas appear in their cells (Excel widens the columns with best-fit so that the formulas appear in their entirety), and long text entries no longer spill into neighboring blank cells.

Excel allows you to toggle between the normal cell display and the formula cell display by pressing Ctrl+`. (That is, press Ctrl and the key with the tilde on top.) This key — usually found in the upper-left corner of your keyboard — does double-duty as a tilde and a weird backward accent mark. (Don't confuse that backward accent mark with the apostrophe that appears on a key below the quotation mark!)

After Excel displays the formulas in the worksheet, you are ready to print it as you would any other report. You can include the worksheet column letters and row numbers as headings in the printout so that if you do spot an error, you can pinpoint the cell reference right away.

To include the row and column headings in the printout, put a check mark in the Print check box in the Headings column on the Sheet Options group of the Page Layout tab of the Ribbon before you send the report to the printer.

After you print the worksheet with the formulas, return the worksheet to normal by clicking the Show Formulas button on the Formulas tab of the Ribbon or by pressing Ctrl+`.

Chapter 6

The Ten Commandments of Excel 2013

● ●

*W*hen working with Excel 2013, you discover certain do's and don'ts that, if followed religiously, can make using this program just heavenly. The following Excel Ten Commandments contain just such precepts for eternal Excel bliss.

10. **Thou shalt commit thy work to disk** by saving thy changes often (clicketh or tappeth the Save button on the Quick Access toolbar or presseth Ctrl+S). To saveth thy file in the almighty cloud so that thou may easily access thy workbook from any of thy computing devices, selecteth a folder on thy SkyDrive.

9. **Thou shalt nameth thy workbooks** when saving them the first time with filenames of no more than twelve score and fifteen characters (255), including spaces and all manner of weird signs and symbols.

8. **Thou shalt not spread wide the data in thy worksheet,** but rather thou shalt gather together thy tables and avoideth skipping columns and rows unless this is necessary to make thy data intelligible. All this thou shalt do in order that thou may conserve the memory of thy computer.

7. **Thou shalt begin all thy Excel 2013 formulas with = (equal)** as the sign of computation. If, however, ye be formerly of the Lotus 1-2-3 tribe, thou shalt haveth special dispensation and can commence thy formulas with the + sign and thy functions with the @ sign.

6. **Thou shalt select thy cells before thou bringeth any Excel command to bear upon them,** just as surely as thou doth sow before thou reapeth.

5. **Thou shalt useth the Undo feature (clicketh or tappeth the Undo button on the Quick Access toolbar or presseth Ctrl+Z)** immediately upon committing any transgression in thy worksheet so that thou mayest clean up thy mess. Should thou forgeteth to useth thy Undo feature straightaway, thou must select the action that thou wouldst undo from the pop-up menu attached to the Undo command button on the Quick Access toolbar. Note well that any action that thou selectest from this drop-down list will undo not only that action, but also the actions that precedeth it on this menu.

4. **Thou shalt not delete, nor insert, columns and rows in a worksheet** lest thou hath first verified that no part yet undisplayed of thy worksheet will thereby be wiped out or otherwise displaced.

3. **Thou shalt not print thy spreadsheet report lest thou hath first previewed its pages by clicking the Page Layout View button** (the middle button of the three to the immediate left of the Zoom slider on the Status bar) and art satisfied that all thy pages are upright in the sight of the printer. If thou art still unsure of how thy pages break, clicketh the Page Break Preview button to its immediate right on the Status bar to seeth how Excel doth divide thy pages.

2. **Thou shalt changeth the manner of recalculation of thy workbooks from automatic to manual** (clicketh Formulas⇨Calculation Options⇨Manual or presseth Alt+MXM) when thy workbook groweth so great in size that Excel sloweth down to a camel crawl whenever thou doeth anything in any one of its worksheets. Woe to thee, should thou then ignoreth the Calculate message on the Status bar and not presseth the Calculate Now key (F9) or clicketh Formulas⇨Calculate Now before such time as thou mayest print any of thy workbook data.

1. **Thou shalt protecteth thy completed workbook and all its worksheets from corruption and iniquities** at the hands of others (clicketh Review⇨Protect Sheet or Protect Workbook). And if thou be brazen enough to addeth a password to thy workbook protection, beware lest thou forgeteth thy password in any part. For verily I say unto thee, on the day that thou knowest not thy password, that day shalt be the last upon which thou lookest upon thy workbook in any guise.

Index